FRENCH EN[TRÉE]
PARIS

A Gatwick *Eat and Sleep* Guide

FRENCH ENTRÉE 11

PARIS

Laurence Phillips

Series Editor: Patricia Fenn

Quiller Press

Hôtel St Merry

Acknowledgements

First to Patricia Fenn for inspiration and guidance and to her daughter Charlotte for much editorial help.

Thanks to the Comte de Valbray for his early research on this guide; to my Parisian friends for allowing me to introduce the British to their secret tourist-free tables; to Chantal and the ladies in the office on the faubourg St Honoré for their help and advice; to all my Paris dining partners – especially to Thierry, and to Frédéric; and to Nicky for her life-saving home-cooked suppers when my spirits were flagging. And most of all to Ronald Phillips, my father, for getting out the car and ferrying me around the final two arrondissements when the clock and the calender said that it could never be done.

First published 1993 by Quiller Press Ltd
46 Lillie Road, London SW6 1TN

Copyright © 1993 Text: Laurence Phillips
Illustrations and maps © 1993 Quiller Press Ltd
Line drawings: Emma McLeod-Johnstone
Maps: Helen Humphreys
Front cover: Tim Jaques

ISBN 1 870948 83 1

Photoset by Townsend Typesetter Limited
Havana House, Sabrina Avenue, Worcester

Printed and bound by Firmin-Didot (France)
Groupe Hérissey - N° d'impression : 23778

Contents

How to Use this Book

1 Nowhere within the Périphérique is more than a short walk from a Metro station. At the end of each listing address in the guide you will find the name of the nearest station in brackets. In the ticket hall of each station is a large scale Plan du Quartier, showing clearly how to find every address in the neighbourhood. A Metro map is available from all hotels, stations and department stores and a simplified street map of the city is free from hotel reception desks.

2 Phone numbers in the listings are for local calls. From outside the Paris region you must first dial the area code [1].

3 L, M or S in the margin stand for Luxury, Simple and Medium. See below for prices.

4 (H) stands for Hotel, (R) for Restaurant, (ST) for Salon du Thé and (B) for Bar in combination with the above reference, ie (H)S, (R)L etc.

5 The ➤ symbol means the establishment fulfils exceptionally well at least one of the author's criteria of comfort, welcome and cuisine. See also page 13.

6 Ⓜ stands for market day.

7 Credit cards: AE = American Express, DC = Diner's Club, MC = Mastercard (e.g. Access), V = Visa. No cc = no credit cards accepted.

8 Hotel prices generally represent a room for two people. The standard room-rate applies to single or double occupancy.

9 Restaurant prices are obliged to include all taxes and service charges.

10 The numbers with the address printed at the head of each arrondissement listing are the postal codes – e.g. 75009 – and should be used in all correspondence.

11 Prices in general: prices quoted in the text were correct at the time of going to press – however, they should be taken more as a comparative guide between entries.

In restaurants, meals in the category 'S' would usually cost under 120f a head – in most cases far less; 'M' suggests a budget between 120 and 250f; 'L' establishments would charge over 250f. Remember that many 'L' establishments offer lunches in the 'M' category.

Hotel prices are a little higher in Paris than the rest of France. As a rule of thumb, an 'S' class hotel will charge under 300f for a room; 'M' prices are between 300 and 550f; 'L' costs soar skywards from here. Remember also that 'M' class hotels may have some rooms or suites in the 'L' category, so do confirm the price on booking.

Foreword

Romantic Paris is a firm favourite with the British and so, not surprisingly, is London Gatwick Airport's most popular destination.

The airport's strong link began on May 17 1936 when a de Havilland DH-86 took off for Paris and a place in aviation history. The passengers, paying the princely sum of four pounds and five shillings (including return first-class rail fare from London) were embarked on the first international scheduled service from London Gatwick which had once been a racecourse and was destined to become one of the busiest international airports in the world.

Now we're strengthening our link further by supporting *Entrée to Paris*, an essential piece of holiday packing for those bound for this beautiful city.

Paris is just one of the many French destinations served by flights from London Gatwick. Working with our airlines and airport-based companies, we aim to ensure travellers receive as warm a welcome at the airport as they find at their final destination.

These days air travel knows no bounds and, there's no doubt about it, flying remains the most exciting way to start a holiday. Our task here at London Gatwick, and all our 'sister' BAA airports, is to give our passengers the best possible service from check-in to take-off. And when it's time to fly home we aim to provide a smooth and efficient end to the journey.

At London Gatwick we have always been at the forefront of passenger aviation and have earned our place as one of the world's premier international airports, handling around 20 million leisure and business passengers a year.

We aim to give passengers the best possible start to their trip to Paris and, aided by this Entrée guide, we're sure their holidays will go on to be an all-round success.

Allan Munds
Managing Director
Gatwick Airport Ltd.

Author's Preface

On my eighteenth birthday I grabbed the key of the door to a city that has called me back home ever since.

The Gare du Nord was a magical wonderland, a noisy fanfare to Paris that greeted the bottle-green boat-train, a clattering, chattering station that sent a city to work and me out to play.

Opposite was the Brasserie for the first coffee of the stay and a few stops down on the Metro was my cheap and cheerful hotel.

Today I touch down in Roissy Airport. Terminal One has the fun glass tubes, Terminal Two a speedy checkout of less than ten minutes. But I still take the train into Gare du Nord for that first intoxicating gulp of Parisian air.

The Brasserie remains (see 10th arrondissement), as does the hotel (see 18th arrondissement). But since that first welcome the city has shown me her other guises.

Parisians try to change their city and like almost no other capital, Paris is constantly being rebuilt; yet it never loses its former identities. Street names – as ever in France – are constantly changed to honour heroes and places. The quaint names of Victor Hugo's Paris have all but disappeared. Still the streets and their spirits remain.

Over the years, I've learned to love each of the many faces of this city. Each district, each arrondissement, each quarter is a Paris quite apart.

The blasé resident of the 16th knows nothing of the villager in Belleville. Can the students poring over books in the cafés of the left bank live in the same city as the scrum lurching into the bargain baskets outside Tati's discount clothes store at the foot of Montmartre?

It takes, perhaps, an outsider to compile an insider's guide to the variety of Paris, so I make no apologies for being a Londoner who happens to call Paris 'home'.

In all this time, and especially over recent months, I have had the joy and privilege of discovering hotels and restaurants that continue to confirm those first impressions of the city: the bedroom that is built onto a working church, with flying buttresses thrust over the bed; the wine-cellar-inspired hotel with a different vintage wine stored in each room; the bistro run by priests in a former sex shop; the great Japanese chefs who are creating a renaissance of simple French regional cooking.

As long as the twenty villages of Paris continue to provide the inspiration, every visit will be my first.

To anyone reading this book and arriving in Paris for the first time or the 100th time: I wish you welcome, a wonderful stay and *bon appétit*.

Laurence Phillips

Author's appeal

In order to keep *French Entrée* up to date I need all the latest information I can get on establishments listed in the guide. If you have any comments on these or any other details that might supplement my own researching I should be most grateful if you would pass them on.

Please include the name and address of establishment, date and duration of visit. Also please state if you will allow your name to be used.

Laurence Phillips,
Quiller Press,
46 Lillie Rd,
London SW6 1TN

How to Use this City

Armed with a copy of the Entrée, a Metro map and a spirit of gastronomic adventure – Paris is your huître.

Public transport is cheap, clean and efficient. Think carefully before buying a tourist ticket. If you are planning on fewer than 10 journeys a day, pick up a carnet of ten tickets. At around 36f this gives you ten individual trips on the Metro, the high speed RER express trains and the cable car at Montmartre.

Tickets can also be used, in clusters of two to three, for bus journeys at street level. Some buses still have open galleries at the back for sight-seeing and exhaust-sniffing.

Using the Metro is simple. Platforms are named after their termini. Follow your route on the map to the end of the line or the name of the platform required, e.g. from Louvre to George V you should take the train marked 'La Défense' and travel six stops.

Your green ticket should be franked by the barrier before boarding the train.

Taking the RER service out of the city centre (for a supplementary fare) you should check out the acronym on the front of your train. Names such as NORA, VERA and VICK refer to suburban stations served.

At your underground destinations blue signs marked SORTIE indicate various exits. Check the Plan du Quartier for the best exit.

Nowhere in Paris is more than a couple of hundred yards from a station and trains run every couple of minutes during the day, so you'll find you need budget around a quarter of an hour for the average trip, door to door.

Minitel, the telephone data service, is used for everything from finding a partner for the evening to timetables and theatre tickets. Tapping in '36.15 SITU' on your hotel's Minitel machine will give you the best route to your destination, with the fewest Metro changes, the shortest walks between platforms, or the least number of steps. Just key in your hotel address and the address of your destination.

Paris is best seen on foot. Designed for the nosy, the city seems to have an unlimited supply of tempting doorways, passages, hidden squares and unexpected views. Although detailed street maps are sold at most news kiosks, a free map showing all main streets and indicating all the sights and quarters of the city is published by each of the main department stores. Pick up a copy at your hotel.

Do please explore. If you've booked a room in one of the more popular quarters, take an afternoon and evening to discover the real Paris across town. The 19th, for example, is almost unknown to tourists, yet has hidden secrets old and new – see the chapter later in the book.

Go to the theatre – there are loads of shows and plays to be seen that do not feature feathers and pancake make-up. Check out the more unusual museums. There is a museum of fakes, a museum of hairstyles and even a gallery devoted to the specs of the famous.

Try to visit one of the older style bistros or bars before they completely disappear. The national sport of Passive Smoking is fading under the pressure of the new laws which forbid smoking in public. You do not realise how much the smell of strong tobacco contributes to the sensation of Paris, until you've eaten a meal and, even as a committed non-smoker, react gratefully to the request, 'Do you mind if I smoke?'

Night buses – called Noctambus – leave the place du Châtelet hourly through the night. They run along every main route of the city and will stop on demand. A special ticket is required.

Paris taxis allow only three passengers to squeeze in the back seat. The front passenger seat is often reserved for the driver's spaniel. Do not expect a sedate purring ride. Each gear change is a macho experience.

Driving is an adventure, and driving around the place de l'Etoile is an activity not recommended by insurance companies who refuse to pay out on accidents in the shadow of the Arc du Triomphe.

Paris closes during July and August. Several of the restaurants listed here are shut for between 2 and 6 weeks during this period. However, as most Parisians choose to leave the city on the weekend after July 14, the streets become gloriously empty thoroughfares for the tootling tourist. You can even park in the streets without fear of reprisals from the blue-clad traffic wardens.

The Champs Elysées are never deserted, whatever the season. The cheery traffic jams of a summer's evening flash yellow and red lights and parp their horns at the shoppers doing the midnight chores and the clubbers tripping from floorshow to dance floor.

One night a year the whole city is en fête. The Fête de la Musique fills streets and squares, cafés and railway stations, as bands, buskers, professionals and passers-by sing and dance till the small hours of June 21st.

There are several other festivals to enjoy. Citywide, the

summer-long Festival Estival de Paris, and the later Festival d'Autumn can be enjoyed all over town. Some quarters have their own local events and these are listed in the arrondissement introductions of the Entrée.

All year is party time past the witching hour in the city centre, from the left bank cafés to the golden belt of the Champs Elysées. Night time bustles in Les Halles and Pigalle, yet can sparkle on the Pont des Arts and the place Hôtel de Ville.

Arrondissement by Arrondissement, District by District

Paris defies mathematics. There are twenty quarters in one Paris and the whole is still greater than the sum of its parts. Some of its parts hide the secrets revealed in this guide.

The city is divided into twenty districts, or arrondissements. These fan out from the centre of town in an escargot-shaped spiral. Each arrondissement has a personality very much its own, and it is the village heart of each district that I have tried to discover.

To most visitors, the arrondissement number means nothing but a cypher printed atop each blue street sign. The traditional quarters of Paris are those names we've known all our lives – Pigalle, Montmartre, the Bastille and the Left Bank.

Many of these traditional areas sprawl over more than one local arrondissement, although the style from one district to another can alter noticeably when you cross a road.

For your guidance, here are the traditional Parisian quarters and where to find them:

Bastille – Officially the 12th arrondissement, but the place itself borders on the 4th and 11th as well.

Beaubourg – The Pompidou Centre is in the 4th arrondissement.

Belleville – 11th and 19th arrondissements.

Champs Elysées – The 8th arrondissement. But remember that the Arc du Triomphe, place de l'Etoile, is shared with the 16th and 17th.

Cité – The Ile de la Cité, with Notre Dame, and the Ile St Louis are both in the 4th arrondissement.

Concorde – 1st and 8th arrondissements.

Eiffel Tower – 7th arrondissement, but on the border with the 15th. The Trocadéro Gardens, for the best view of the Tower, are actually in the 16th.

Grands Boulevards – Mainly the 9th (for the big department stores) but also the 2nd, 3rd and 10th arrondissements.

Les Halles – The former street market, now a commercial and entertainment centre is to be found in the 1st arrondissement.

Latin Quarter – 5th arrondissement – see Rive Gauche.

Louvre/St Honoré – The heart of the 1st arrondissement.

Le Marais – 3rd and 4th arrondissements.

Montmartre – 18th arrondissement.

Montparnasse – Shared between the 14th and 6th, but the 7th and 15th fall under the shadow of the Tower itself.

Opéra – The boulevards and neon signs of the Moulin Rouge and other late night attractions take in the 9th and 18th arrondissements – see Montmartre.

République – The boulevards fan out through the 3rd, 10th and 11th arrondissements. The place de la République is mainly in the 11th.

Rive Gauche, The Left Bank – Takes in the 5th, 6th and 7th arrondissements, from the Tour d'Argent to the Musée d'Orsay.

In Search of the Cheap Bistro

Ou sont les cheap bistros d'antin? The legendary three-course meal for the price of a bottle of house wine is an endangered species. The Parisian brasserie has been saved from extinction by the Flo chain, which has lovingly refurbished, nay resuscitated, the great brasseries of the city, the Flo, Coupole, Terminus Nord and Vaudeville among them. Boffinger, in the 4th, was rescued by the revival of the Bastille, and the Charlot seafood bar kept alive by the nightlife of Pigalle.

As to the simple tables where locals go for boeuf bourguignon and a pichet of red wine, these have lost favour to the fast food invasion, and the yuppy designer eateries.

Still, there remain several addresses where no one can dine for more than 50 or 100f. Those recommended in the Entrée listings include this baker's dozen:

1st arr -	**Aux Deux Saules** – not what it was, but still offering an inexpensive snack lunch in Les Halles.
4th arr -	**Le P'tit Gavroche** – lunch and dinner, three courses for around 40f.
5th arr -	**L'Epoque** – menu under 60f served in the evenings by a young and committed team.
6th arr -	**Polidor** – eat well for under 100f away from the tourist traps of the quarter.
7th arr -	**Chez Germaine** – with individual courses from less than 10f, there's change from 50f for a full meal in this no-frills room. **Thoumieux** – pay around 60f for a nourishing meal in this noisy student-favoured canteen.
8th arr -	**L'Entrecôte** – Salad, steak and frites, with the famous Café de Paris sauce for less than 80f – and practically on the Champs Elysées as well!
9th arr -	**Chartier** – legendary soup kitchen where you can spend under 50f, and 80f buys a banquet.
13th arr -	**L'Espérance** – solid workman's lunches for under 50f.
14th arr -	**Rendez-vous des Camionneurs** – real Routier's red meat meals at around 60f.
15th arr -	**Le Commerce** – you won't need a 100f note to eat well in this haven in a pricey quarter.
17th arr -	**Iwi des Mers** – lunch from around 60f and dinner under 100f.
19th arr -	**La Chaumine** – rough and ready food from the Limousin at under 50f. **Rendez-vous de la Marine** – a 50f main course is as good as a feast in a most welcoming bistro du port.

The back streets of every quarter will all offer at least one local bar serving lunches of the pâté, coq au vin, tarte maison variety. Don't expect gastronomy, just nutrition, for around 50f. Even the rue Casanova behind the place Vendôme has its cheap lunches. Parisians tend to opt for the foreign restaurants when it comes to cheap lunching. Chinese, Greek, Italian and North African meals come out at well under 50f a head.

The Grandes Tables

How can the Entrée call itself a guide to Paris without a listing for the Tour d'Argent? La Tour d'Argent is arguably one of the world's greatest restaurants. The view across the Seine is unrivalled, the wine cellar legendary. To most of us, the bill is also a myth.

At over 1,000f for dinner, and the cheapest set lunch menu at 450f, it is quite simply not an Entrée establishment.

For years, the French Entrée series has introduced its readers to the simple and the lavish, the humble logis and the grand château. All establishments share the distinction of providing value for money within a recognisable budget.

In this guide I have searched, sniffed and snuffled like a truffle hound, to find in the capital those restaurants and bistros typical of France that Pat Fenn has been showing us around the country for years – those reliable standbys, those absolute treasures, those time-capsules and those other-worldly secrets.

Most tourists find the obvious eateries. And everyone knows the legendary tables. This Entrée seeks something in between.

Thus the Tour d'Argent, Lucas Carton and even Maxims (with its defiant policy of refusing to post its menu prices outside the restaurant) do not appear in here.

You know them already and Michelin and Gault Millau already say enough about them to make any extra listing here superfluous.

Where we have detailed one of the classic tables it is because of a special value menu, or perhaps because a deserved reputation might not yet have crossed the Channel.

However, no guide would be complete without a list of the best expensive addresses. Should you wish to visit any of these restaurants for a very special occasion, be prepared. You are practically guaranteed excellence at these places – but do budget around 600-1,000f a head.

1st arr - **Gérard Besson**
5 r. du Coq-Héron, 42 44 14 74.

5th arr - **La Tour d'Argent**
15-17 qu. de la Tournelle, 43 54 23 31.

6th arr - **Jacques Cagna**
14 r. des Grands Augustins, 43 26 49 39.

7th arr - **Arpège**
84 r. du Varenne, 45 51 47 33.

Jules Verne
Eiffel Tower, 45 55 61 44. ·

8th arr - **Lucas-Carton**
9 pl. de la Madeleine, 42 65 22 90.
Taillevent
15 r. Lamennais, 45 63 39 94.
Le Bristol
112 r. Faubourg St Honoré, 42 66 91 45.

14th arr - **Le Duc**
243 bd. Raspail, 43 20 96 30.

16th arr - **Faugeron**
52 r. de Longchamp, 47 04 24 53.
Robuchon
32 r. de Longchamp, 43 26 49 39.
Le Pré Catalan
Bois de Boulogne, 45 24 55 58.
Le Clos Longchamp
Hotel Méridien, 81 bd. Gouvion-St-Cyr, 40 68 00 70.
Vivarois
192 av. Victor Hugo, 45 04 04 31.

17th arr - **Michel Rostang**
20 r. Rennequin, 47 63 40 77.
Guy Savoy
18 r. Troyon, 43 80 36 22.

Special Recommendations (Arrows)

1st arr -   Le Petit Bourbon (R)SM
             Chez Denise la Tour de Montlhery (R)M
             Serge Granger (R)M

2nd arr.   Le Célador (R)L
             Pile ou Face (R)ML

3rd arr -   Hôtel des Chevaliers (H)M
             Ambassade d'Auvergne (R)M

4th arr -   St Merry (H)M
             Bretonnerie (H)L
             Hôtel du Jeu de Paume (H)L
             L'Ambroisie (R)L
             Le Maraîcher (R)SM
             Le P'tit Gavroche (R)S
             Café Beaubourg (R)S

5th arr -   Le Jardin des Plantes (H)M
             Select Hotel (H)L
             Hôtel Esméralda (H)M
             Les Colonies (R)M
             Le Coup Chou (R)M

6th arr -   Relais Saint Germain (H)L
             Hôtel St Paul (H)M
             Hôtel St Michel (H)S
             Joséphine, 'Chez Dumonet' (R)L

7th arr -   Duc de St Simon (H)L
             Nevers (H)M
             Le Divellec (R)L
             L'Arpège (R)ML

8th arr -   George V (HR)L
             Les Suites St Honoré (H)L
             Hôtel de l'Elysée (H)M
             L'Entrecôte (R)S
             Yvan (R)M

9th arr -   Chartier (R)S
             Le Petit Batailley (R)M
             La Table d'Anvers (R)ML

11th arr -	Astier (R)S
	Chez Fernand/Les Fernandises (R)SM
12th arr -	Au Trou Gascon (R)ML
	La Gourmandise (R)ML
	La Sologne (R)M
13th arr -	Résidence des Gobelins (H)M
14th arr -	La Cagouille (R)M
	La Régalade (R)SM
15th arr -	Le Clos Morillons (R)M
16th arr -	Caveau des Echanssons (R)S
	Faugeron (R)L
17th arr -	Hôtel de Banville (H)L
	Iwi des Mers (R)S
	Epicure (R)SM
18th arr -	Le Restaurant (R)M
19th arr -	Rendez-vous de la Marine (R)S
	Pavillon Puebla (R)ML
	Au Cochon d'Or (R)ML

Is There Life After Confit de Canard?

Foreign Cuisine in Paris

Is there life after confit de canard? Is there more to Paris than a panaché des poissons served with a julienne of miniature vegetables and followed by a chaud-froid of summer fruits in their coulis of early berries and a crème anglaise?

Of course there is. Paris is a cosmopolitan city, and French cuisine is but one course on the capital's menu gastronomique. Scores of national dishes vie for the attention of the locals, and all styles, from Hungarian to Haitian, Korean to Kosher, are served all around town.

This Entrée has concentrated on the traditional French tables of Paris, but it is worth remembering that the newer international trends are soon picked up by the kitchens of many of the city's classic restaurants. L'Epicure 108 in the 17th arrondissement, and La Sologne in the 12th, both benefit from their highly talented Japanese chefs, and, even in the St Honoré district, Bernard Chirent takes an oriental approach to his moules and fresh fish. The popular left bank restaurant Les Colonies has a new team in the kitchen treading a culinary tightrope of Sino-Gallic creativity.

Although pizza and paella are not what we would associate with a romantic weekend in Paris, an international dinner excursion may be just the ticket during a longer visit to the City of Lights (sweetmeats and rognons de veau).

It is worth noting that the best Japanese food is served in the 1st between the Grands Boulevards and the rue St Honoré: sushi specialists run along the north side of the Louvre and Falais Royal. Chinese and Vietnamese cuisine is the speciality of the 13th and is to be found in the outlying arrondissements, along with North African restaurants for cous-cous. Algerian and Lebanese cuisine is usually to be tasted along the Grands Boulevards, and in the Goutte d'Or area of the 18th.

Kosher restaurants are located around the Folies Bergères and the rue Faubourg Montmartre in the 9th, as well as the centuries-old Jewish quarter in the Marais (try the rue des Rosiers). They can also be found, surprisingly enough, by the abattoirs of La Villette.

Greek restaurants line the pedestrian streets such as the rue de la Huchette, behind St Michel on the left bank.

Italian food is highly respected. In Paris you will have the best Neopolitan meal outside Napoli, undoubtedly the finest Italian restaurant being Chez Vincent on the rue St Georges in the 9th.

British tea drinking is taken seriously – The Tea Drinkers' Club of Paris meets at the George V, and there are even fish and chip shops.

Of course America is represented – and not simply by the fast food joints on every street corner, nor the fifties-style diners of Les Halles. The US regions are fêted by Bob Payton's Chicago chain, and the French-owned Marshalls introduced Californian cuisine to the 8th.

Don't think about Indian meals in Paris – very expensive, and quite disappointing. When entertaining a chic Parisian in the UK, a local tandoori house will be regarded as a gastronomic treat.

Paris Hotels

What is a typical Paris hotel? For some it is the garret room with its skylight looking out over the roofs of the Left Bank or Montmartre. Others dream of champagne and bubble bath, and a view of the Eiffel Tower. Both fantasies are reality, and between the two are the two-, three- and four-star options of any modern European destination.

For Entrée readers the standard city-class hotels and executive suites of a business capital have no place in their travel plans.

I have sought those rooms that Pat Fenn has discovered around the country – the rural lodging houses and provincial châteaux, family-run establishments where the grandmother mows the lawn and the niece waits at table. I have endeavoured to uncover hotels of charm and personality within the capital's city limits.

Arrondissement by arrondissement, quarter by quarter, the streets of Paris have yielded their secrets. Of course, the charms of the city are very different to those of the countryside. Where a one-star logis in the heart of the countryside might offer cosy luxuries, its twin on the left bank of the Seine might have threadbare towels, creaking floorboards and no lift. But the view of Notre Dame, the sound of a fiddler in a late-night café or the smells of a street-market bring something uniquely Parisian.

At the other end of the scale, de luxe is something far more vivacious than the château elegance of a country estate. The flair of the St Honoré or Champs Elysées is revealed in the wit of a Chanel creation, the sparkle of a purchase from the place Vendôme, and the click of an elegant heel on a marble step.

There are no five-star hotels in Paris. Since the taxation of the crème de la crème hotels was increased to ruinous levels, hoteliers at the highest level asked for their establishments to be downgraded. As one of the city's leading hoteliers retorted, 'We don't need stars; our name sparkles more than the stars.' In between are hotels where the decor will not offend (anyone with memories of the psychodelia of the last great decoration spree in the sixties will remember the bright and floral wallpapers of some Paris hotels), the hot water tap will deliver the goods, service will be attentive, and noisy streets will be silenced by decent windows and doors.

There's more than a sprinkling of hotels associated with the greats of the past, and a few that are the secret haunts of today's discreet legends.

Hotel prices in Paris, as in the rest of France, are per room not per person. Slight variations in charges sometimes occur to take into account extra bed linen and breakfasts. Some of the larger hotels have special peak and low season rates. It is always worth checking at the time of booking whether a premium charge is being made.

At certain times of the year booking is essential – at all grades of hotel – as the city's business life takes over its tourism role. During the fashion weeks, the motor-show and major trade fairs, rooms at all prices are snapped up. The Paris Air Show, held in June every odd-numbered year, can fill up every hotel bed in the city.

The published room rate can often be discounted. The best value deal in the city is the annual Bon Weekend à Paris promotion. Running from the beginning of November until March, Bon Weekend is an annual promotion offering two nights for the price of one on stays commencing on Friday or Saturday nights. Around 100 independent hotels of all grades from two star to four star de luxe are involved in the campaign. A list of participant hotels is published each autumn by the French Government Tourist Office. Reservations should be made eight days in advance, and guests receive a book of vouchers entitling them to two-for-one deals on sightseeing tours, boat trips, shopping and other attractions.

Many of the hotels in this Entrée offer their own similar deals during the low season. Larger luxury hotels such as the George V and the Lutétia offer year-end room, shopping and meal packages at well below the usual accommodation rates.

For weekenders planning a trip from UK airports other than London, independent package options from companies such as Travelscene and Kirker can offer accommodation at certain Entrée-listed hotels together with air transfers at rates far below the separate room and flight prices.

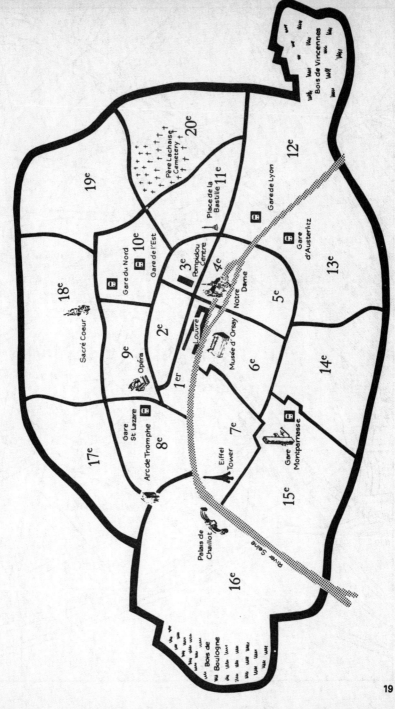

Bois de Vincennes

12e

Gare de Lyon

Père Lachaise
Cemetery

20e

Place de la
Bastille 11e

Gare
d'Austerlitz

13e

19e

Gare du Nord 10e
Gare de l'Est

Pompidou
Centre 3e 4e

Notre
Dame

5e

18e

Sacré Coeur

9e
Opéra

2e

Louvre

Musée d'Orsay 6e

14e

1er

Gare
St Lazare

8e

7e

Gare
Montparnasse

17e

Arc de Triomphe

Eiffel
Tower

15e

Palais de
Chaillot

River Seine

16e

Bois de
Boulogne

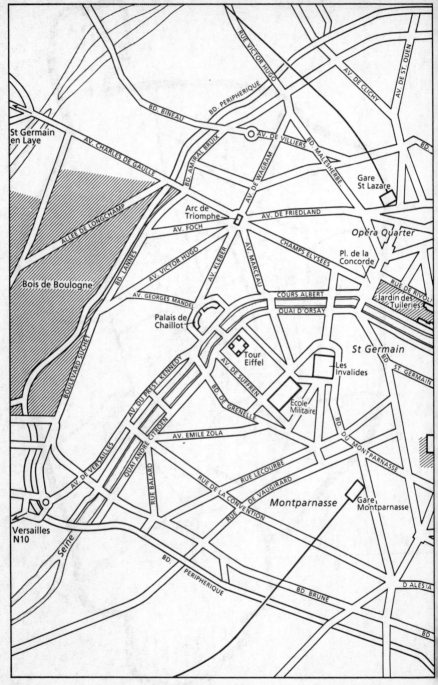

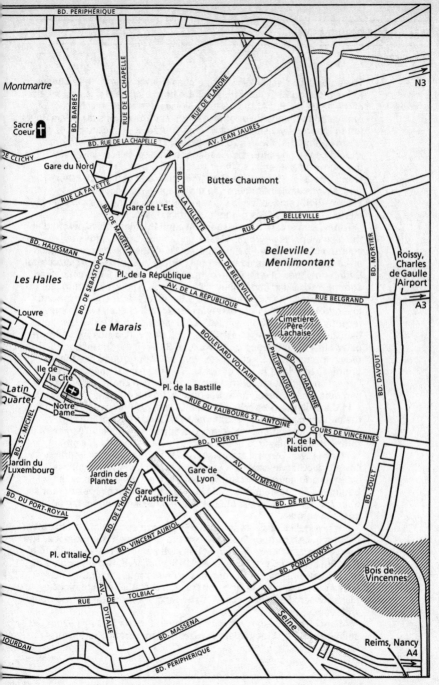

1st ARRONDISSEMENT

(Paris 75001)

The Louvre–Les Halles district stretches from the place de la Concorde to the place du Châtelet. The southern border is the Seine and the tip of the Ile de la Cité. At the north, the place Vendôme, recently renovated to Mansart's original design, and the jardins du Palais Royal (often ignored by visitors, but a good spot for a picnic snack).

How fitting that the centre of the snail spiral of arrondissements should be the one-time royal seat – the Louvre Palace. This vast museum and garden is so large that there are four metro stations along its walls. You can take the train from one end to the other! The ride is worthwhile, if only to see the imaginative decor of the Louvre–Rivoli station, once the main entrance to the Louvre, with its platform reproductions of the museum's treasures.

Today, one enters the museum through the giant glass pyramid at the next stop, Palais-Royal-Musée-du-Louvre. Don't judge the controversial structure by the photos. Of all the grands projets, such as La Défense and the new national library, this is the most successful. Sitting on plates of water, the pyramids turn the classic architecture and the Paris skies into a giant kaleidoscope. Midweek, during late night opening, the night lights of Paris reflect into the underground foyer. In 1993, the Louvre extends along the Richelieu wing, until recently the home of the Ministry of Finance. With the civil servants banished to their new futuristic home at Bercy, this side of the former palace has been opened up to visitors. By 1996 the Grand Louvre redevelopment will be complete, with an underground city that promises to bring the arts of the fashion industry to the world's largest and oldest museum. From here one can comfortably reach the two other main museums at Beaubourg (in the 4th) and Orsay (7th).

In the Tuileries gardens, a funfair is held in summer and midwinter, the enormous ferris wheel offering unrivalled views of the city.

Paris' popular shopping area is the Forum des Halles. The site of the former central market of Paris is now the fast food, flash clothes centre of town. Several storeys of underground galleries with the city's videotheque waxwork and hologram museums, countless cinemas and a huge swimming pool matched at street levels by boutiques and restaurants. Many are designer br-uncheries or tourist traps but some retain the old market traditions of onion soup and snails at sunrise.

For Les Halles has always been the place to end a night on the town. Since the 12th century this has been the city's main market place. The famous iron and glass market houses were built in the second half of the 19th century. They have, alas, all disappeared. But something of the romance of the market remains. Where pretty, rich girls once flirted with Gauloise-puffing porters, you can still find late night bistros where Parisians, rather than tourists, choose to confuse dawn with dusk.

All manner of flesh is served here along the rue St Denis – the culinary variety at the table, the more vibrant carnal offerings in doorways and pavements. Unlike many of the city's red light districts, the St Denis has an improbable stagey feel. The bright costumes and carefully applied maquillage of the streetgirls have a well-polished Hollywood sheen

The rue St Honoré was once one of Paris' main streets. Today traffic crawls along. The wider parallel thoroughfare of the rue de Rivoli whisks traffic from Bastille to Concorde past the shops, department stores and grand hotels. The St Honoré has its prohibitive boutiques and furriers, expense account restaurants for those in the jewellery or fashion business, and occasional surprisingly convivial café.

A dull grey car park on the place du Marché St Honoré stands guard over the next gastronomic treat of the district, an up-and-coming crossroads of restaurants to watch.

And all a short stroll from the arcades of the Tuileries stretch of the rue de Rivoli.

Booksellers (bouquinistes) on the banks of the Seine, near Châtelet. Birds and animals sold on the opposite side of the quai de la Mégisserie.

HOTELS

Hôtel Meurice
(HRST)L   *228 r. de Rivoli, 44 58 10 10, all cc (Tuileries)*

It was the Calais Postmaster, Augustin Meurice, who decided in 1817 that British VIPs needed a luxurious hotel in Paris after travelling 36 hours in his post-chaises. Even today, nothing beats flinging open a tall bedroom window and looking across the Tuileries to the Orsay. A true Palace hotel, silence behind the Rivoli clamour: pampered, polished, furnished and refurbished to glorious effect. The Louis XV style salon de thé, hosted by an enormous portrait of Madame de Pompadour, is an experience for the eyes, ears and taste buds. The restaurant: a sparkle of crystal and silverware; a generosity of cut flowers; a young anxious staff darting from table to table; and music by a pianist whose hands are the feet of Fred Astaire, yet whose face has the discretion of a deputy chairman of a modest building society. Michelin's star to chef Marc Marchand is, I feel, premature. He has imagination in creating a menu, but his team does not yet carry the ideas to the plate – bland truffles, flour and water sorbet. Lunch 300f. A la carte 500f. Rooms from 2,500f, but special weekend offers.

Molière
(H)M   *21 r. Molière, 42 96 22 01, all cc (Palais Royal)*

Opposite the Molière fountain, and just a dramatic gesture away from the Comédie Française is this popular Opéra district hotel. A graceful oval staircase betrays the building's history as a private house and –

don't be misled by the name – the home of one of France's great writers. But not Molière – this was once chez Voltaire, who first gave private performances of his work in this very building. Nonetheless, Molière is fêted by the pictures in the hall. A good base for the classic museums and sites, being a brief stroll away from the new Louvre, barely 10 minutes from the Orsay and on the most central metro line, which strings the Pompidou Centre, Les Halles and the Champs Elysées together.

If it is somewhat top heavy with English-speaking guests, that can be excused because so many of them work with the fashion houses, so the gossip and scandal at breakfast is an eavesdropper's delight. Breakfast comes at 35f for the traditional variety, and there is a modest buffet of yoghurt, cereal and fruit for an additional 15f. The style of the ground floor breakfast salons is what I would call hearty-arty; they are in fact art galleries, with exhibitions from fashionable artists, though the garish paintings displayed during my stay were inclined to bring on indigestion. With rates in the region of 500f one expects and receives the usual extras: mini-bar, bathroom goodies, hair-dryer and international TV channels. You draw the short straw if your room number ends in a 3 or a 4, but the ones and twos are charming, with quaint en suite bathrooms, and the fives have bathrooms big enough for a modest dinner party! Service is never less than smiling and helpful.

Résidence la Concorde
(H)L   5 r. Cambon, 42 66 38 89, all cc (Concorde)

Unlike the better known hotels of the rue de Rivoli, Monsieur Saada's discreet three-star establishment is hidden from view. There is no street level entrance or reception. Pass through into a small private courtyard and take the little lift to the third floor reception. From around 700f, rooms are modern and well fitted (number 44, octagonal with corner alcoves, is my favourite) and bear no resemblance to the little rabbit hutches that the present owner inherited when he bought the hotel 17 years ago. Breakfast is served in the neat little morning room and bar, and a display case in reception shows off the unusual jewellery created by a friend, Mila Mareckova. Helpful staff and an unpretentious haven in the bustling Concorde-Tuileries quarter.

Agora
(H)S   7 r. de la Cossonerie, 42 33 46 02, MC V AE (Châtelet-les Halles)

It could not be more conveniently located for the visitor afraid of missing a second of the bustling lights and excitement of this trendy city. Straight up the escalator from the metro's most central interchange and you are there. The eclectic first floor reception is cluttered with paintings, caged birds and bric-à-brac ranging in style from the charming, through kitsch, to downright naff. Staff are friendly and helpful and the rooms vary from the bright and balconied on the second floor, to the 6th floor garrets with skylight views of the rooftops of Les Halles and the bustling streets. Not for those seeking complete bed rest, as this noisy quarter has restaurants and clubs open until 5 am. Prices around 300f.

Britannique
(H)M   *20 av. Victoria, 42 33 74 59, all cc (Châtelet)*

The Avenue Victoria from Châtelet to the Hôtel de Ville is arguably the centre of Paris. All the city's nightbuses depart and return here, and the charms of the Marais, Les Halles, Ile de la Cité, Left Bank and the Louvre fan out from here. The hotel is tucked away at the quiet end of the street just opposite the Théâtre du Châtelet, where play big American musicals and operas from *Hello Dolly* to *Porgy and Bess* and good operatic productions as well. The Britannique was a Quaker mission during the First World War; today it is an inoffensively decorated warm-leather-style peaceful base, with helpful staff. Some rooms are rather compact for 600f, but all are clean and well fitted.

Le Lion d'Or
(H)S   *5 r. de la Sourdière, 42 60 79 04, no cc (Tuileries)*

A bargain off the St Honoré. A double room with shower for not much more than 200f. No lift, loos in the corridors and no bar. But a warm welcome, a pile of English and French magazines and paperbacks in reception and a superb location in the heart of town make this an Entrée candidate.

RESTAURANTS

➤ **Le Petit Bourbon**
R(SM)   *15 r. du Roule, 40 26 08 93, cc, AE V MC, cl Sun eve and Mon (Les Halles)*

Les Halles is hardly the Parisian famine district, with more fashionable restaurants per square napkin than anywhere else on the right bank. However, take away the pizza parlours, American diners and burger bars, and you have a minefield of the fashionable and the touristic. New eateries open almost by the minute, so when an opening comes with an established pedigree, the bewildered visitor can be assured of a special evening. Michel Derbane was the toast of Montmartre with his restaurant Chants de Piano [see 18th arr.]; now he brings his delicate touch to the rue du Roule. Imagination and attention to detail are Derbane's hallmarks, and Les Halles has been wooed and won by such dishes as rognons de veau aux grains de café grillés. The culinary flamboyance of the 230f menu dégustation is equally evident on the main carte-menu at 140f. Arrowed for a welcome and value to be treasured in a district which often promises, but only occasionally delivers.

➤Chez Denise la Tour de Montlhery
(R)M   5 r. Desprouvaires, 42 36 21 42, MC V, cl Sat, Sun, 14 July-15 Aug, open 24 hours a day (Les Halles)

> Eating times are irrelevant to Denise Benariac and husband Jacques whose delightful bistro in the heart of Les Halles is open all day, all night. This is the incarnation of the true Parisian bistro – jugfuls of table wine, wafts of Gauloises, high-decibelled chatter, waiters twisting deftly between red-and-white-clothed tables. Food is unpretentious – well under 200f for a generous helping of chicken liver pâté, steak and a rich chocolate mousse. Perhaps it is the simple menu which puts off the tourists – clientele are nocturnal Parisians who recognise a good genuine bistro when they see one. An arrow for authenticity and atmosphere.

➤Serge Granger
(R)M   36 pl. du Marché St Honoré, 42 60 03 00, all cc, cl Sat lunch and Sun (Pyramides)

> Tomorrow's upmarket response to Les Halles is an unlikely concrete multi-storey car park. The monstrosity is just off the rue St Honoré and place Vendôme and, according to our waiter, is soon to be replaced by something more aesthetically pleasing. So, little by little, the shops around the square, and along the tangential rue Gombost, are being taken up by restaurateurs. A turn around the square offers a range of eateries to suit any taste from the assured classic Grille [see below] to the trendy brasserie Batifol [see below also]. A fair selection of modest and pretentious bistros, a smattering of cafés and wine bars, and a healthy portion of Japanese restaurants complement the original parades of North African and Chinese establishments. Serge Granger is not the best known of the St Honoré chefs, but he is fast gaining respect amongst those Parisians lured up the staircase by an unassuming, inexpensive menu. Granger's is typical of a good restaurant in a small town. Perhaps his years as a private caterer and pastry-chef encouraged him to retain the old ways when he opened this, his first Parisian restaurant. Both the young and the more mature waiting staff offer helpful advice on the menu, and tend to steer diners towards the fish. The catch from St Malo arrives in the kitchen to be prepared simply but with careful attention to texture and flavour. Excellent light and delicate sauces. A simple smoked salmon mousse serves as an appetizer, but don't be put off ordering meat – the same deft hand is at work in the kitchen. My dinner guest, himself a former bistro chef, had nothing but admiration for the tender entrecôte steak with chive butter. We both agreed that the desserts were a revelation. My nougat glacé was honeyed to perfection, and the gentle crackle and melt of fine filo pastry from the other plate was musical. Granger himself takes a low-key tour of honour at the end of the evening and everyone, from the waiter to the caissière downstairs at the till, asks how we enjoyed the meal.

Serge Granger

Batifol
(R)S   *12 r. du Marché St Honoré, 42 60 47 21, V MC (Pyramides)*

Very bright smart decor as befits tomorrow's trendy venues. After all a
Flo Prestige lies just the other side of the square. This is the latest
branch of Batifol, the most famous residing in the shadow of the Tour
d'Argent on the boulevard St Germain. An interesting clientele. Just in
our corner of the large dining room, we had a swarthy Gauloise-
puffing priest who looked like a mariner straight out of Genet (we
strongly suspected tattoos under his cloth); next to us was a terribly
trendy post-opera quarter; nice young girls with their boyfriends had
the other table and across the way, a table of drunken workmen
insisted on wearing their napkins as makeshift wimples. No menu as
such, but a very reasonably priced brasserie menu. Don't expect
genius in the kitchen – the money went on the decor. But rillettes and
a pot-au-feu were adequately prepared for a round midnight jaw-
session. My noisettes du thon were pleasant enough, and an

inexpensive wine list brought dinner to around 120f per head. Service was inconsistent, from the friendly to the downright cavalier. The fly in our ointment was the cork in the carafe, and a waitress who shrugged off our complaint.

Les Cartes Postales
R(M)   *7 r. Gombost, 42 61 02 93, MC V, cl Sun Aug (Pyramides)*

In all the Japanese restaurants of the quarter can be found the most fashionable of Parisians. Decor is simple, as the name suggests: glass-covered postcards adorn the walls; foie gras with a spicy kick and aromatic variations on seafood themes keep the 190f menu from chef Yoshimasa Watanabe full of surprises. The wine list lacks the imagination of the menu. A la carte can stretch the budget to around 400f.

A la Grille St Honoré
(R)M   *15 pl. du Marché St Honoré, 42 61 00 93, all cc, cl Sun, Mon, Aug (Pyramides)*

This is the classic restaurant of the new quarter. Very traditional dishes. Rabbit, duck and veal are prepared to perfection, vegetables fresh as can be and wines surprisingly inexpensive for the calibre of restaurant. A la carte can cost between 300-400f. However, there is a limited menu at around 200f.

Bernard Chirent
(R)M   *28 r. Mont Thabor, 42 86 80 05, V MC, cl Sat lunch, Sun (Concorde)*

Pictures from antique recipe books grace the walls of this fashionable restaurant sandwiched in a quiet street between the noisy St Honoré and Rivoli thoroughfares. Chirent has a deft wit and subtlety in his 'Cuisine Actuel', keeping a weather eye for current fads and incorporating them into a classic repertoire. Witness the masterly use of thyme in both the Japanese influenced émincé of thon cru in a soy-based marinade and the soupe des moules. Mussels in various guises are something of a house speciality and lunchtime sees the fashionable suits and cashmeres of the St Honoré district bent over bowls piled high. Desserts too warrant attention; a marbled chocolate soufflé in particular is a highlight of the summer menu. Allow 400f if dining à la carte. Menus at around 170f and 250f include wine.

Carre des Feuillants
(R)L   *14 r. Castiglione, 42 86 82 82, all cc, cl Sat lunch, Sun (Tuileries)*

In a striking glass-enclosed courtyard of the Castiglione arcade off the place Vendôme, is the principal home of restaurateur Alain

Dutournier. A menu Idées de Saison has five courses at 500f (with four wines 700f) per person and à la carte could cost the same. The specialities of the Relais Gourmand dining room include such enticing suggestions as a barigole de poivrades et d'escargots (petits gris escargots presented with violet artichokes) and a daube de taureau aux premiers cèpes. But the prices, and the fact that the menu is printed in English, make this less of a typical Entrée suggestion. Entrée readers seeking bon rapport quality-prix and unpretentious country warmth are urged to take the metro or taxi across town to the 12th arrondissement, where M. Dutournier's second restaurant, Au Trou Gascon, is arrowed for bringing the welcome and flavours of his beloved south-western France to the capital.

Angélina

(ST)L   *226 r. de Rivoli, 42 60 82 00, all cc, open 9.30 am-7 pm daily (Tuileries)*

The ultimate salon de thé. The decor – stucco columns, Belle Epoque frescoes, gilt mirrors – is as delectable as the pâtisseries. Students, businessmen, the 'BCBG' (bon chic bon genre – French for yuppy) brigade, the famous, the infamous and those in search of fame all patronise Angelina. They come for what is surely the wickedest hot chocolate in town (32f), for a Mont Blanc, a delectable concoction of gooey meringue on a crisp nutty base, piled high with frothy Chantilly, or perhaps a delicate pâtisserie masterpiece. For the guilt-ridden, there are salads available from 60f.

Le Grand Vefour

(R)L   *17 r. de Beaujolais, 42 96 56 27, all cc, open 12.30-2 pm and 7.30-10 pm, cl Aug, Sat lunch, and Sun (Palais Royal)*

One of those 'once in a lifetime' places – reserve Le Grand Vefour for that extra special occasion. One look at the decor, the menu and the prices explains why. Even in its former guise as the Café de Chartres, no. 17 rue de Beaujolais – almost a part of the Palais Royal – has always attracted the rich, the famous, the aristocratic, even the rulers (Napoleon and wife Josephine came here) of French society. Many have declared this the most beautiful restaurant in the world. It's hard to disagree, depending on how much you value the gold and gilt, the flowers, the silks, all reflected five times over in extravagant mirrors. As the bill will reveal, no expense is spared. Service is irreproachable, there when you want it, smiling and unobtrusive. Prime ingredients are cooked imaginatively, 'nouvelle' in conception but not in quantity. Our 'sole sur le plat' served with a sauce of moules followed by bitter chocolate soufflé were sublime. It's not easy to keep the wine prices down here but the young sommelier advises well. Prices range from the good value (relatively speaking) 300f menu to around 700f à la carte.

Chez la Vieille
(R)M   *37 r. de l'Arbre Sec, 42 60 15 78, no cc, lunch only, cl Sat and Sun (Louvre)*

'La Vieille' refers more to the unpretentious, traditional cuisine than to the age of its owner, Madame Biasin, whose long list of loyal customers means that her eight tables are hard to come by (advance booking essential). This is French country cooking (with a strong Lyonnaise influence) at its heartiest best. Long-neglected dishes from rural France like succulent terrines, stuffed tomatoes, beef stews, all simple dishes so frequently spoiled elsewhere, are the norm. Prices may seem steep for the decor and simplicity of the menu (count on 300f) but authenticity rarely comes cheap.

L'Escargot Montorgueil
(R)M   *38 r. Montorgueil, 42 36 83 51, MC AE V, cl Mon and Aug (Les Halles)*

Right in the heart of Les Halles, rue Montorgueil is lined with trendy boutiques, chain cafés, tourist rip-offs ... and the Escargot Montorgueil (you can't miss the big snail sitting above the restaurant). This is *the* place to snail-sample and has been for over 150 years. Even if you're not into snails, go for the scenery – stunning 1830s bistro style. Red and black predominates, between gilt mirrors; an elaborate wrought-iron staircase spirals up to the first floor and in the entrance hall are ceilings taken from Sarah Bernhardt's private dining room. Supervising is Madame Saladin Terrail (sister to Claude of Tour d'Argent fame). Service is brisk and not particularly friendly. No need to point out the speciality – served every way imaginable – 'au curry', 'à la provençale', 'au roquefort' – some more successful than others. The four course 240f dinner or 140f lunch includes snails, a meat and fish dish and good crème brulée. Go for the setting ... and perhaps the odd escargot.

Au Pied de Cochon
(R)M   *6 r. Coquillière, 42 36 11 75, V MC AE, open 24 hours a day 365 days of the year (Les Halles)*

It would take a braver man than I to ignore the last of the Les Halles dawn-farewell favourites. Here, having danced the night away, romantics linger with the sunrise, before returning home to the smell of fresh croissants. Most Parisians, at some stage in their lives, will have started or finished their day at Au Pied de Cochon. They'll go there to sample some of the best onion soup in town and a plateful of grilled pig's trotter – the house speciality as the name implies. Unfortunately, Au Pied du Cochon has of late become a victim of its own success. All the guides classify it as 'typically Parisian' – which is true, but only when all the tourists have returned to their hotels, making way for the nocturnal Parisians. If you do decide to go before 3 am, reservations are a must. Noise level is high, especially before the 2 am night buses, and service is brisk. Summer dining recommended. Allow 250-350f to eat; beware wine prices which have shot up noticeably in the last couple of years.

Café Jean Nicot
(R)S   *173 r. St Honoré*

> Unsophisticated, fifties-style frescoed café, good for spying on the St
> Honoré shoppers – this is designer land after all. Regulars prop up the
> bar all hours of the day over a 'Calva'. Bar snacks only, starting at 15f.

Minim's de Paris
(ST)L   *76 r. du Faubourg St Honoré (Concorde)*

> As its name implies, a lesser, cheaper version of neighbouring
> Maxim's: very kitsch, very touristy, but it does allow the budgeter to
> experience the Maxim's glory without putting too big a hole in his
> wallet. Food is uninspired, standard brasserie dishes.

Aux Deux Saules
(R)S   *91 r. St Denis, 42 36 46 57, V MC, open noon-midnight (Châtelet-Les Halles)*

> A victim of its own success, alas the wooden benches and shared
> tables of five years ago have been 'upgraded' with run-of-the-mill
> restaurant terrace furniture. The old menu, too, has been made more
> tourist 'friendly' by the new management. However, the beautiful tiled
> Belle Epoque decor of this long time Les Halles favourite can still be
> admired – and if you hunt carefully on the menu, you can tuck into the
> boudin blanc, country pâté and omelettes, and fill up on three courses
> for well under 100f. Most important of all, the legendary onion soup
> can still be supped on the pavements of this sleazy street.

L'Amazonial
(R)SM   *3 r. Ste Opportune, 43 33 53 13, V MC AE, open until 3 am (Châtelet-Les Halles)*

> A predominently young and flamboyant Les Halles crowd enjoy noisy
> and animated dinners at this ever popular and fashionable Latin
> American styled dining room and terrace. Reliable modern menus
> with good fish and pâtés invariably incude at least one low calorie
> option for each course. A 78f menu is served early in the evening;
> after 9 pm only the 98f menu applies. With wines, budget around 200f.
> A la carte can be around 300f.

Café Costes
(B)L   *4 r. Berger, 45 08 54 39, no cc, open until 2 pm (Châtelet-Les Halles)*

> For the trendy, the only place to sit in to see and be seen. The Philippe
> Stark decor is much appreciated by the clientele – very much the same
> type who frequent the Café Beaubourg in the 4th – who are happy to
> pay more than double the usual price for a coffee. Arrogant waiters
> wear dinner jackets, denims and a regulation sneer, but the futuristic
> toilets (2f) have to be seen to be believed. Pricy.

2nd ARRONDISSEMENT

(Paris 75002)

Above the 1st arrondissement and below the grands boulevards of the Capucines, Italiens, Montmartre, Poissonnière and Bonne Nouvelle is this wedge of the business district. The 2nd takes on aspects of the style of its neighbouring quarters. The opera house, in the 9th, gives the boulevards a raffish air, the riches of the 1st boost the banking world based here in the 2nd, and the food and frolics of the Faubourg Montmartre area make the tables worth a visit.

Before the reign of Louis XIV, what we know today as the grands boulevards were the city walls and at Strasbourg-St-Denis we can still see the old city gates, Porte St Denis and Porte St Martin. As Paris grew, these walls became wide thoroughfares, where Parisians would take the air, strolling, sitting, people-watching.

As time passed, theatres opened along the boulevards – even today, they remain the southern tip of theatreland. At the less fashionable East End (today's 3rd arrondissement) were the circuses to the west came Opéra. The boulevard des Italiens gets its name not from an early desire to promote a united Europe (in fact France's first plan for a non-federal Europe was made by Napoleon), but from the incessant stream of popular Italian opera flowing from the Opéra Comique.

And where music played, dandies were made, flamboyant fashions were constantly paraded along the boulevards, as Haussmann's dramatic sweep through the city, from the place de l'Opéra to the place de la République, became the place to be seen.

Today's dandies might patronise Jean-Paul Gaultier's outrageous showroom, fashionably unfashionably located here, in the rue Vivienne, rather than the couture district of the 8th. Otherwise, the wide Haussmann streets are lined with brasseries and a few modest shirt shops. In the evenings, however, as tables are filled with theatregoers, and the nightclubs and fashionable discotheques prepare to open their doors at midnight, the grands boulevards bring a touch of excitement to a district whose daywear is the sober suit appropriate to the Banque de France, the Bourse and the offices of financial institutions and airlines.

Truthfully, the nightclubs are across the boundary in the 9th, but some of the theatres are in the 2nd. Whatever the postcode of the main attractions, the 2nd has the cafés and brasseries to serve the revellers, when the locals are fast asleep.

HOTELS

Lautrec Opéra
(H)L   *8 r. d'Amboise, 42 96 67 90, V MC AE (Richelieu-Drouot)*

If the name fails to give it away, the Jane Avril surplus in the reception area should tell you that this was, once upon a time, the home of Toulouse-Lautrec. Of course the hotel, in a small but noisy street, is

Opéra Comique

substantially better kept than was the building known by the artist, whose appartment was on the first floor. Don't bother asking for *the* room. It no longer exists as such. Instead enjoy the hotel on its own merits. Double rooms cost between 550f and 900f on average, and there is an excellent choice of styles. My own favourite is number 63 with its own wooden staircase to the bed under the eaves. Here one can play artist's garret to one's heart's content, secure in the knowledge that today's garret comes complete with mini-bar, safe and hair-dryer. Rooms at the end of each corridor have lovely stone walls and plants perched in unlikely nooks. Others have pretty pink or blue fabrics on the walls and are altogether more feminine. Some of the second floor bedrooms have improbably high ceilings making a small double airy and comfortable. It goes without saying that the pictures in each bedroom – regardless of decor – are copies of *those* posters.

Hôtel Mariveaux
(H)M   *10 r. d'Amboise, 42 97 56 58, all cc (Richelieu-Drouot)*

> Next door to the Lautrec, here you'll find smart and stylish modern decor in modest-sized rooms with all the facilities expected of a city centre three star. The hotel was renovated just a couple of years ago, and is a comfortable stopping point in the Grands Boulevards area, but off the boulevards themselves. Don't choose a window facing the front, if you like a mid-week lie-in. The little rue d'Amboise may be nothing more than a side street to the Opéra Comique by night, but the city's taxi drivers have all discovered the perfect rat-run in which to sound their horns during the day.

RESTAURANTS

➤**Le Célador**
(R)L   *15 r. Daunou, 47 03 40 42, all cc (Opéra)*

> Joel Boilleaut is chef de cuisine and as such is responsible for the treats served in the peach and green dining rooms of the Celador restaurant at the Hotel Westminster. Large plates and wine glasses await the serving of such delights as pigeon et caille au pistou sous la peau, rôtis au four, whose texture and flavour did justice to the anticipation ignited by the detailed title. Diners at a nearby table had ordered the lasagne du homard au basilic and the aromas wafting in our direction seemed equally worthy. I love a good cheese selection, and the choice here was served with home-made walnut and raisin bread. A nougat glacé in an autumn fruit coulis more than sufficed as a suitably sweet finish to a memorable dinner. That is until I'd crisped a fork into the snappy and delicious millefeuille chosen by my guest. And wished I could start all over again. A la carte comes to around the 500f mark, but the set menu is 300f.

Le Vaudeville
(R)M   *29 r. Vivienne, 42 33 39 31, all cc (4 September)*

> Like the Flo, another grand brasserie rescued from the lapse into oblivion, the Vaudeville is exactly what its name suggests – an eatery for boulevardiers en route to a rollicking comedy at the Théâtre des Variétés. Truth be told there are as many refugees from the Bourse opposite as bon vivants, but no matter. What does matter amidst the potted plants, polished brass and faux marbre of the brasserie decor is the food. And for around 160f my summertime menu included an excellent gazpacho, both creamy and crunchy, a perfectly acceptable escalope de saumon, that was salmon in flavour as well as colour (no mean achievement in a boulevard brasserie these days) and, to conclude, a soupe des fraises that was a veritable trove of the tiniest sharpest little wild woodland strawberries ever to be tamed by a sensible sorbet.

→**Pile ou Face**
(R)ML   *52 bis r. Notre-Dame-des-Victoires, 42 33 64 33, V MC, cl Sat, Sun, Aug,*
Christmas (r. Montmartre)

It is good stuff, you know, the foie-and-farmyard fare, served in the
one-time neighbourhood restaurant that was discovered by a wider
public and in turn discovered higher prices. The pity has always been
that a bill between 400-500f per head means that one has to ration
visits to the traditionally crimson and gold dining room. Rich
businessmen and prosperous visitors splash out on pigeonneau rôti à
l'huile de truffe, followed by rich chocolatey desserts. The cellar is well
up to the standards of the kitchen, but recession-consciousness has
penetrated even this corner of pricey-dining, and for the first time the
Pile ou Face has created a carte-menu. It is finally possible to dine
here for 235f, and thus we can happily hand over an arrow for value
and quality.

Les Noces de Jeanette
(R)M   *14 r. Favart, 42 96 36 89, all cc (Richelieu-Drouot)*

The sturdy blanquette de veau à l'ancienne and the andouillette
AAAAA [that's Association Amicale des Amateurs des Andouillettes
Authentique to you and me] sets the tone for the sort of après-theatre
restaurant that the Parisians would term 'agréable'. Les Noces graces
a corner site opposite the opéra comique and the restaurant's own
style, with its retro dining rooms and lovely old mirrored staircase, is
straight out of an operetta. The place was conceived by the
proprietors of Montmartre's successful Crémaillère, and has the same
atmosphere of a shared joke: we the diners as well as the waiters are
playing at Belle Epoque. A pretty pretence with reliable fare, good
natured service and a menu at 159f.

Victoria Station Wagon Restaurant
(R)SM   *11 bd. Montmartre, 42 36 73 90, AE NC V (r. Montmartre)*

The name is English, the decor is pullman carriage kitsch and they
serve pizza – what is this place doing in this Entrée? Calm down, and
I'll tell you that every morning and afternoon the smell of freshly
chopped firewood being carried through the restaurant is but a hint of
the heady perfume to come. For, despite the railway theme, this is a
Parisian rarity – a restaurant that boasts an open real wood burning
stove where dishes are prepared in the dining room itself. Besides the
pizzas, the restaurant does a good line in simple, unpretentious steaks
and grills. The restaurant is almost opposite the Musée Grévin
waxwork museum and some tables have a view into the Passage des
Panoramas – one of the charming arcades of the quarter.
Pay 100-150f.

Les Noces de Jeannette

Chez Georges
(R)M   *1 r. du Mail, 42 60 07 11, AE MC V, cl Sun (Bourse)*

Eavesdropping is the speciality of this favourite bistro, for the journalists, bankers and brokers of the 2nd arrondissement dine elbow to elbow in front of a row of imposing arched mirrors. Lunchtime secrets find their way from the Bourse to the city pages, via hefty chucks of turbot in a sauce bearnaise and good fillet steaks. Wines are reasonably priced and a good old-fashioned meal should set you back around 250f.

Le Grand Colbert
(R)M   *2 r. Vivienne, 42 86 87 88, AE MC V (Bourse)*

> A classic brasserie, with decor that extends beyond the frescoes and mosaics to the very costumes worn by the waiters of yesteryear. Restrain yourself from singing the second scene of La Bohème and enjoy standard fare. Old reliables such as the frisée aux lardons, poule au pot and a reasonably priced steak tartare – under 80f. The house whiting is prepared to a 300-year-old recipe. Budget around 200f with wine. Open from breakfast onwards, with last orders taken at 1 am. Very convenient for the Comédie Française.

Le Gramont
(R)M   *15 bd. des Italiens, 42 97 58 50, NC V (Richelieu-Drouot)*

> Café, brasserie, salon de thé, the Gramont with its sneak view of the Sacré Coeur up the hill has been there for me through the years. A typical pavement café of the Grands Boulevards, the wide thoroughfares of banks, kiosks and occasional fast food bars. Poule au Pot dinners served in the brasserie until well past midnight have often assuaged those post-theatre hunger pangs. Lunch is under 100f, evening meals around the 150f mark. Coffee on the pavement at all hours.

Harry's Bar
(L)   *5 r. Daunou, 42 61 71 14, open daily from 11 am-4 pm (Opéra)*

> An intrinsic part of the Parisian landscape. A preserve of the international *élite*, the rich and famous, those who have 'made it' and know they have. Businessmen congregate on the ground floor to talk share prices and Wall Street; couples take refuge in the more intimate basement, over a Blue Lagoon or Bloody Mary. Cocktails aren't too astronomical – the simpler varieties start at 50f.

Tarte Julie
(ST)M   *17 bd. Montmartre*

> The simplest ideas are always the best, as the Tarte Julie chain demonstrates. No. 17 bd. Montmartre is as reliable as the others found dotted around the capital. Each shop cooks on the spot – sweet, savoury, fruity, creamy, fishy and always fresh.

3rd ARRONDISSEMENT

(Paris 75003)

The Marais means literally the Marshland, as this area once was a
slushy bog, to the north of the island that was Paris. The right bank,
above the Ile de la Cité was uninhabitable until the 13th century, when
the swamps around the rue St Antoine, were converted to farmland.
Gradually, as the area was built up, the Marais became a fashionable
alternative to the city centre. In the late 14th century it even became a
royal retreat for Charles VI. The Marais encompasses today's 3rd and
4th arrondissements.

The 3rd is the top of the former marshland. The northern Marais
quarter from the rue Rambuteau, above the Pompidou Centre and
place des Vosges, to the grands boulevards fanning from République,
is one of those districts that has been given a second life since the
1960s. Culture, the Musée Picasso, the national archives, and the
Conservatoire des Arts et Métiers, shares the streets with the Sentier –
the wholesale clothing district, that spills over from the north of Les
Halles.

It has its less successful corners: the area to the north of the
Pompidou Centre is the Horloge quarter, a modern cluster of shops
that is seedy despite all attempts to present it as chic.

The joy of the Marais lies in its many secret courtyards. The hôtels
particuliers are grand private residences whose high street gates hide
some stunning entrances. Worth a visit are the Hôtels Carnavalet,
Salé, Rohan and Soubise. The buildings are floodlit at certain times of
the year. The square du Temple is very much the heart of the
arrondissement for the locals, with unpretentious bars and grills
serving market staff and residents. With the attractions of République
and Bastille to the east, Les Halles to the West and the shops and
cafés of the southern Marais all a short walk way, this remains both
central yet tranquil – a city centre rarity.

*Covered market, Tue-Sat, 8 am-1 pm, 4-7.30 pm, Sun 8 am-1 pm:
Enfants Rouge, 39 r. de Bretagne (Filles-du-Calvaire).*

HOTELS

Pavillion de la Reine
(H)L   *8 pl. des Vosges, 42 77 96 40, all cc (St Paul)*

The only château-style hotel of this quarter in the appropriate setting
of the Queen's pavillion in Paris' most beautiful square. Not quite a
château, but with rooms and salons fitted very much to the style, the
air-conditioned grand siècle comfort is served to the well-heeled who
can afford the 1,100-2,950f per night rooms. No bar, but drinks are
served in the imposing main salon, or in the bedrooms, via the quaint
trompe l'oeil lift. A tiny courtyard garden is a charming bonus but the
true delight is a base on the lovely pre-Revolution square where

English nannies push prams on a summer's morning, and some superb restaurants and salons de thé are just a stroll along the arcades. Private parking within the hotel.

➤Hôtel des Chevaliers
(H)M   *38 r. du Turenne, 42 77 96 40, all cc (St Paul)*

An arrow for the genuine welcome at Ghislaine Truffaut's cosy Marais hotel. As you step inside this one-time private house of the 16th century – just around the corner from the place des Vosges – the two tiny Yorkshire terriers greet you as a long lost friend. Detaching your shoelaces from the canine doormen, check into your room. Discreetly modern decor with valet stand, hair-drier, cable TV and mini-bars. On each pillow rests a petite box of sweets, and at the bedside a little basket of fruit. The welcome extends throughout your stay. Ghislaine spent years in the rag trade before setting up the hotel five years ago, and she will steer guests away from the conventional department stores to the truly Parisienne boutiques and shops. Her enthusiasm for her hotel, guests and neighbours is infectious; many clients become penpals. Once a month she organises a wine tasting and art show in the breakfast cellar. Breakfast at 40f is a full buffet by the way – once the site of an auberge in the days of the royal tournaments. Future plans include musical evenings and expanding the reception. The hotel has just 24 rooms and many look into the tiny trellissed well of a courtyard. British guests prefer the top two floors with their rooms under the eaves. But it is the charm of the hosts rather than the decor that makes the Chevaliers special. During a recent metro strike, Ghislaine's father was pressed into service running an unofficial taxi service ferrying guests around town.

Marais
(H)M   *2 bis r. des Comminies, 48 87 78 27, all cc (Filles-du-Calvaire)*

Clean, if plain, rooms facing into the courtyard. Plastic and silk flowers brighten the foyer, and relaxed staff are keen to help and advise guests on facilities in the quarter and the city in general. Just a short walk to the Musée Picasso and the place des Voges. Rooms from 360f with bath.

RESTAURANTS

➤Ambassade d'Auvergne
(R)M   *22 r. du Grenier-St Lazare, 42 72 31 22, MC V, cl end July (Rambuteau)*

The trendies of the Marais-Les Halles may have stormed the Bastille, but the family-run embassy of all that is glorious in the Auvergne is made of stronger stuff. So the decor remains, all creaking timbers and potent foods to whisk the visitor back to those tables we have all discovered along unlikely lanes in the heart of rural France. The best ham in the district, according to wiser counsel, and real food, such as

duck daube and a cassoulet you could stand a spoon in, continue to
delight. The aligot is my weakness, a knockout potato dish with garlic
and heady cantal cheese. The bill should set you back around 250f.
Don't be clever. Ask the waiter to recommend an auvergnat wine for
your meal. The fairly priced cellar includes much unknown outside the
region. Long may the Petrucci family preside over this treasure house.
Arrowed for warmth of welcome and authentic country cuisine.

Chez Jenny

Chez Jenny
(R)M   *39 bd. du Temple, 42 74 75 75, AE V MC, open 11 am-1 am (République)*

Queen of the choucrouteries – style, ambiance, staff and cuisine are all
straight from Alsace. The interior makes much of lace, polished wood

and ornate lights, and the upstairs marquetry is fine. You may prefer to sit outside watching the République revellers hit town. Service is brasserie-style and brisk, but usually friendly and willing to advise. Portions are colossal and dishes rarely return scraped clean. If you're unfamiliar with choucroute, this is *the* place to try your first but don't stray too far from the original version – variations on the theme are less recommended, though the fish variety is acceptable to non-meat eaters in the party. Prices are reasonable with a 180f menu, guaranteeing a full stomach. The famous house choucroute is 70f, and the apéritif maison is made with beer – picon sirop de citron and bière d'Alsace is under 30f. The Vosgienne meringue isn't too heavy unlike the delectable house speciality – gâteau de fromage blanc, as rich and wicked as it sounds. Alsatian wines make good companions to the heavy food – a pitcher of Gewürztraminer washes everything down nicely. The place gets absolutely packed at weekends.

4th ARRONDISSEMENT

(Paris 75004)

The more bustling and ever-developing heart of the Marais is the southern section, below the museums and workshops of the 3rd. The 4th arrondissement, with France's most popular museum, the Pompidou Centre in the west, the places des Vosges and de la Bastille in the east and the two islands in the Seine marking the southern limits, is one of the liveliest and most varied districts in the capital.

In front of the Pompidou Centre at Beaubourg hundreds of visitors gather to picnic on the cobbles, enjoy street entertainers, watch the seconds to the year 2000 tick away on the huge digital millenium clock and be unashamedly touristy. The atmosphere is still that of Les Halles across the way. A deliciously silly collection of fountains cools the crowds and there is a year round carnival atmosphere.

Behind the controversial museum, all is much quieter. This is the southern Marais which, since the area's renovation in the 1960s, has attracted a fashionable element whose penthouse apartments overlook the old streets where shopfronts now are more likely to display Matisse prints or pricey cufflinks than meat and vegetables. Café theatre flourishes here, and one can still see top stars performing in off-beat cabaret venues.

The trendy Marais rests remarkably comfortably alongside the older ghettos. The Jewish district around the rue des Rosiers has hardly changed in decades. The oldest square in Paris, the place des Vosges, is one of the few remaining pre-Revolution squares in France: the former place Royale has 36 houses forming a symmetrical pattern of arcades. Good food is served here, and antiques are sold on the pavements of the colonnades. The Pavillon du Roi, on the south side, was once a royal residence. It faces the Pavillon de la Reine, now a hotel, to the north. Victor Hugo's former home on the square is now a museum dedicated to France's greatest novelist. In the gardens, families perambulate with their children and solo tourists relax with a good book.

Across the rue de Rivoli is the southernmost section of the Marais. Hôtels particuliers and the Church of St Paul-St Louis are worth a visit. Once upon a time the area around St Paul was a hotch-potch of trestle-tables piled with bric-à-brac and second-hand goods. Now the stalls have been replaced with pretty little antique shops – and bargains are far less likely to be found.

The islands are the true centre of Paris. This is where the city started, after all. The Gaul fishermen founded Lutetia around 250 BC, building a settlement on the largest island in the river Seine. When Rome conquered the island in 52 BC, Paris was born, on the Ile de la Cité. Until the Middle Ages this island was Paris, and became the French capital in the 9th century. The growth of the universities and churches on the left bank of the river began the expansion of Paris, but the Cité remained for centuries the seat of parliament and justice.

Of course the most famous building on the island is the cathedral of Notre Dame. The rose window and Sunday afternoon organ recitals lure the camcorder classes to one of the most magnificent churches in the world. On this site the first pagan settlers worshipped – their altar is still beneath today's church – the present building took 200 years to complete, finally achieved in 1345. The place du Parvis is the place for that classic view of the cathedral, as seen on tea towels and the big screen.

To the left of the coaches disgorging their passengers and the souvenir hawkers on the Parvis is the Hôtel-Dieu, my personal sanctuary from the hustling, bustling pilgrimage. The hospice, founded in the 7th century, was rebuilt in the late 19th century. Still a working hospital, the cloisters are a haven of tranquillity for a hassled visitor to Paris.

Behind the cathedral, under the gardens of the square Ile de France, is an even better-kept secret – the Memorial of the Deportation. Underground, at the very tip of the island, is the cellar from which victims of the Nazis were deported.

The Palais de Justice, the wonderful Gothic Sainte-Chapelle and Marie Antoinette's prison cell at the Conciergerie are all essential places to visit. Any itinerary should include the places Lepine for the flower and bird market and Dauphine for timeless tranquillity.

The other island, the Ile St Louis, is too often overlooked by visitors who flock to the more obvious attactions on the Cité. Originally two islands, the Ile aux Vaches and the Ile Notre Dame, the two were artificially linked in the 17th century by architects who won royal permission to create a new fashionable district linked by stone bridges to the city's banks. There are quiet streets, expensive shops and a number of high priced, secluded hotels for the discerning visitor to explore.

Flower market, Mon-Sat, 8 am-7.30 pm, pl. Louis-Lepine, Ile de la Cité (Cité). Sunday bird market on the same site, 8 am-7 pm.

Festival de Musique en l'Ile, July-September. Fête du Maray, June – theatre, concerts and exhibitions.

HOTELS

➤ **St Merry**
(H)M   *78 r. de la Verrerie, 42 78 14 15, no cc (Hôtel de Ville)*

The St Merry is unique and one of the most unusual hotels you'll ever visit. Its interior is part of the exterior of the 16th-century church of St Merry standing next to the futuristic Pompidou Centre. Converted 30 years ago from a bordello in the 17th-century presbytery, the flying buttresses of the church plunge through bedroom 9 – surely the most

Hôtel St Merry

original hotel room in the world – and the decor is unbelievable. Glorious 19th-century Gothic furniture and fittings have been assembled by the owner, M. Crabbe, so that each of the 12 rooms is a Gothic fantasy in its own right. Even the first floor foyer has a confessional for a phonebooth. Room 12, with its view of the Tour St Jacques square, is the perfect place for a passionate re-enactment of your Arthurian fantasies. Each of the rooms, priced at 400-900f, is decorated individually. M. Crabbe has been known to close a bedroom for six months until just the right furniture can be found. Bathrooms are definitely of the 20th century and fully fitted. Breakfast served in the rooms is 40f. There's no lift, no television and the hotel takes no credit cards, but the welcome is wonderfully hospitable and the atmosphere unique. Arrowed as my favourite bolt hole and time capsule. Advance reservation essential.

➤ Bretonnerie
(H)L   22 r. Ste Croix de la Bretonnerie, 48.87.77.63, all cc (UK cheques), cl August (Hôtel de Ville)

A quarter of a century ago when the Sagot family first bought this hotel, it was a modest one-star establishment in one of Paris' less salubrious districts. But, with the Marais' leap in fortunes, the Bretonnerie has kept up with its own constant programme of renovation – which is why the hotel closes for a month each summer. The latest move was the leasing of the concierge's room from the building next door, which enabled the family to open up the bare beams of the reception. The oldest part of the hotel, the stone-walled 17th-century building, is furnished with repro Louis XIII. The new wing – leased from next door – is decorated in the style of Napoleon III. Favourite rooms include 34, a 300-year-old garret with *chien assis* windows which offers luxury under the eaves with real Marais charm. 17 is almost a mini suite with its tiny plant-filled balcony, and embroidered bedstead. Mme Sagot buys tapestries in Paris and furniture from Brittany. M. Sagot regrets the disappearance of community spirit amongst the Marais hoteliers – his and the St Merry are the last of the old school. He is quite happy to accept payment in sterling or UK cheques. However, I suggest a courtesy phone call if you are planning to pay this way. Rooms are charged at 600-750f a night. Mini-bar and standard luxuries included. Arrowed for the welcome and style.

Axial Beaubourg
(H)M   11 r. du Temple, 42 72 72 22, MC V (Hôtel de Ville)

Once upon a time, along this road that divides the Beaubourg and Marais quarters, there was a charming run-down little one-star hotel called the Unic. It had a long walk to the upstairs reception, tiny little rooms and ricketty shutters, but it had real character and warmth. Then one day it closed, and after a while the three-star Axial Beaubourg opened with en suite bathroom, colour TV and a new ground floor reception. But the welcome is coolly efficient and the standard class hotel, though clean and modern, is less Marais bohemian and more Beaubourg tourist. Room rates around 470f.

Vieux Marais
(H)M   *8 r. de Plâtre, 42 78 47 22, V MC (Hôtel de Ville)*

This reliable address, with its friendly staff and clean rooms, has been a long-time favourite with all of us who've known the quarter since before gentrification. Modest and welcoming, the hotel has the necessary comforts to make it a popular compromise between the budget one-stars and luxury three-stars of the Marais. Book well in advance – the regulars like to keep the place to themselves. The prices now reflect the area. Rooms around 500f.

➤ Hôtel du Jeu de Paume
(H)L   *54 r. St Louis en l'Ile, 43 26 14 18, all cc (Pont Marie)*

Walking down the quiet main street of the less touristy of the central islands of the Seine, pass through the archway into the 17th-century courtyard and you have to admit that this is one of Paris' more imaginative conversions. The former royal jeu de paume – or indoor tennis court – provides a unique interior decor for the visitor bored with efficient whitewash and chrome. A glass lift affords a superb view of the court and its galleries, cleverly fitted as comfortable breakfast and lounge areas, and the centuries old beams of the court grandly support this airy central well. All the rooms are differently fitted, mod cons and bathrooms *comme il faut*. Ten of the rooms under the eaves have little private spiral staircases to the sleeping area. The hotel also boasts its own sauna. Rooms cost in the region of 800-1000f, breakfast a somewhat steep 70f.

Les Deux Iles
(H)L   *59 r. St Louis en l'Ile, 43 26 13 35, no cc (Pont Marie)*

A glass enclosed courtyard is the centrepiece of this charming and cosy old style hotel. Rooms have attractive blue-and-white-tiled bathrooms and are comfortable country-style refuges for the city-lagged visitor. A welcoming reception-lounge and homely cellar are places to linger after a day's shopping. Room rates are 600-700f. The neighbouring Hotel Lutèce, at number 65, is a slightly higher priced annexe.

St Louis
(H)M   *75 r. St Louis en l'Ile, 46 34 04 80, no cc (Pont Marie)*

Modern bathrooms, attractive if somewhat cramped bedrooms and a warm welcome at this elegant little island hotel, well stocked with antiques and atmosphere. The room rate of around 500f is not too bad for this pricey district. Only the fit should accept rooms on the upper floors – there is no lift.

Place des Vosges
(H)M   *12 r. de Birague, 42 72 60 46, all cc (St Paul)*

> It's not actually in the place itself, but just off the southern arcade. A
> 400f a night mid-range hotel with most of the comforts, TV-free
> rooms, and no frills bathrooms. A courteous welcome in the spacious
> reception leads to the adventure of the lift, designed for one small
> person with half a small case. Guests are given the front door key as
> the hotel is locked up at bedtime.

RESTAURANTS

➤L'Amboisie
(R)L   *pl. des Vosges, 42 78 51 45, V MC, cl school holidays in Feb and Aug (St
Paul)*

> Arrow-awarding is always hardest at the top of the ranks where
> there's more than just the food to consider. L'Ambroisie, however,
> really does excel in the lot: location, decor, interest, atmosphere,
> service ... and the food. The location is in Paris' most elegant square –
> place des Vosges; the decor belongs more to a country château than a
> city restaurant – high ceilings, intricate mouldings, walls adorned with
> tapestries, chandeliers. The welcome is professional but warm,
> likewise the service – both food and wine waiters know their stuff.
> Food is uncomplicated, classic French cuisine with 'nouvelle' touches,
> based on the enhancement rather than disguise of the principle
> ingredients. The marbre de foie gras and the feuillantine de
> langoustines aux graines de sésame have a loyal and enthusiastic
> following. Allow 600f. Wine prices can easily push this up higher.

➤Le Maraîcher
(R)SM   *5 r. Beautreillis, 42 71 42 49, no cc (St Paul or Bastille)*

> Valentin Corral, the owner of Le Maraîcher has put a lifetime of
> travelling and studying into this pretty restaurant. His days as an
> interior design student are reflected in the decor (note the exquisitely
> embroidered napkins and exotic flowers). His Spanish origins bring
> Iberian elements into his highly imaginative menu; his past as a
> sommelier in Bordeaux influences much of the interesting wine list
> And yet, despite his talents, Corral has kept his prices low. His 95f
> menu buys two memorable courses and wine. We lunched on a
> mousseline of St Jacques in a sauce of langoustines followed by
> magret de canard cooked in honey and spices. Five star food at two
> star prices earns Le Maraîcher an arrow. My only criticism is the
> atmosphere – unnecessarily stiff and formal. Otherwise a winner.

Mark Annibal de Coconnas
(R)M   *2 bis pl. des Vosges, 42 78 58 16, all cc, cl Mon, Tue, New Year (St Paul)*

For those who cannot afford the worthy 600f-plus it takes to dine along the square at l'Ambroisie, Coconnas is an alternative dining room on the place itself. After all, it is the baby of Monsieur Tour d'Argent himself, Claude Terrail. Interior decor is the usual velvet, lace and mirrors, but in the season one should sit out under the most beautiful arcades in Paris. After all this is the last remaining square of the *ancien régime*, and should be savoured. Summertime sees the solid wooden dining room furniture augmenting the usual exterior whicker seats. Unfortunately the restaurant has been discovered in recent years, and waiters slip into Italian and English at the drop of a vowel; presenting grubby menus to diners would not have been tolerated in the old days. But with a lunch menu at 120f, this is still something of an old style oasis in a trendy district. A salad printinière with asparagus and melons to augment the expected crudités was encouraging, and the croustillant de saumon was professional enough. The Rocamadour de l'huile d'olive makes a not-too-savoury alternative to desserts. For evenings eat à la carte for 350f and sample the house speciality – poule au pot du bon Roy Henri.

Au Franc Pinot
(R)M   *1 q. de Bourbon, 43 29 46 98, V MC DC, cl. Sun, Mon (Pont Marie)*

Patrice Guyarder's cooking is the only real reason to eat on the Ile St Louis. Slow service and low lighting add to the historical mood of the place. But the pleasant atmosphere generated by a good wine list and M. Guyarder's magical light touch is relaxing enough for that not to matter. Sauces allow such workaday staples as chicken and duck positively to sing to the taste buds. Good value menus at 165f lunchtimes and just 195f in the evenings, mean that such deft cuisine is generously made available even to those who might baulk at the island's pricey reputation.

L'Eglatine
(R)S   *9 r. de la Verrerie, 48 04 75 58, V MC, cl Sun, Mon, Aug (Hôtel de Ville)*

The southern Marais has, over the past decade, developed into Paris' Greenwich Village, bringing with it an inevitable string of precious and posey eateries. I'll never forget the British Colonies Tea Room, a claustrophobic Merchant Ivory nightmare of Englishness, thankfully no longer with us. The memory can still bring me out in a cold sweat! However, alongside the trendy restaurants have appeared some gems, two of which, Aux Mauvais Garçons and the Composite, have sadly disappeared, but the Eglantine remains. The two women who reign in this petite pastel-painted dining room glide silently and efficiently through the evening. So calm are they that, though the place is always packed, it never feels oppressively busy. We spent the evening debating whether the service was unhurried or just slow. This is a favourite place for an evening's catching up on gossip with old friends. Dependable food, served in a relaxing environment. The three menus offer an imaginative choice of dinner; the cheapest at just 64f is served until 10 pm; the others are 95f and 135f. On my last visit we opted for the middle-range menu. An intelligent low budget alternative to the chevignol chaud offered at the top price is a salad of warm gruyère, camembert and chèvre. And the feuilleté of spinach and salmon actually tastes the way salmon used to taste. Escargots are a reliable alternative. The confit de canard was slightly stunned by its brutish sauce aux poivres. Desserts brought a chocoholic choux pastry. One word of warning – don't eat downstairs. At the foot of the stone well lies purdah.

Joe Goldenberg
(R)M   *7 r. des Rosiers, 48 87 20 16, all cc (St Paul)*

In the very heart of the old Jewish quarter is the restaurant (unfortunately best known for a terrorist attack some years ago) that is the only place to be on a Sunday lunchtime. Not what the Americans call glut-kosher, the traditional Jewish dishes are served with ironic insolence that is part of the entertainment at kosher deli-restaurants the world over, from Wolfes in New York to Blooms in the East End. Sitting at the bar taking a healthy interest at the take-away trade in falafel and gefilte fish, or at the tables in the back being served large plates of steaming goulash, the Marais snobs take a day off from being trendy to gossip and dine with the locals. Pay in the region of 200f.

Bofinger
(R)M   *5/7 r. de la Bastille, 42 72 87 82, all cc, open until 1 am (La Bastille)*

One of Paris' oldest brasseries and a Parisian institution since opening its doors in 1864. Regulars come to this bustling brasserie with its sumptuous period decor for the ambience rather than the food. Citizens of the worlds of politics, media, fashion, entertainment and, since the opening of the Bastille Opéra, music, are much in evidence. A good 160f menu often includes foie gras, choucroute, and a spectacular vacherin of strawberries and blackcurrants. Not the place for an intimate meal à deux – tables are close together and it's difficult not to catch a large part of your neighbour's conversation.

Pain, Vin, Fromage
(R)M   *3 r. Geoffroy-l'Angevin, 42 74 07 52, V MC, cl lunch (Rambuteau)*

Three pillars of France allow the cheese-lover to play with the tastebuds. Interesting platters of regional cheeses can mix and match with good strong wines. But cheese is not just a one-course wonder. Although there is no menu as such, you can budget 150-250f for an evening meal, or have just a main course at about 85f. Of course, in winter, there are fondues as well. Patient waiting staff steered me through delicious indecision.

→**Le P'tit Gavroche**
(R)S   15 r. Ste Croix de la Bretonnerie, 48 87 74 26, no cc, cl Sat lunch, Sun,
summer lunches (Hôtel de Ville)

> This tiny backstreet bar with its restaurant tables on all floors is the
> last genuine corner of the pre-yuppy Marais: three course lunch for
> around 40f and dinner for a couple of francs more. A choice of three or
> five main dishes of the coq au vin and simple casserole variety,
> sandwiched between a pâté and a tarte maison. Even if you go à la
> carte you won't pay much more than 100f for the food. Spend your
> small change on a beer or pichet of wine (10f), or knock back a calva
> or cognac with the locals at the bar – a good old-fashioned Paris zinc.
> Arrowed for the miraculous prices.

Aux Enfants Gâtés
(R)S   43 r. des Francs Bourgeois, 42 77 07 63, MC V AE, open weekdays 12 noon-
7 pm, Sat/Sun 12 noon-4 pm (St Paul)

> Shop then flop. Along one of the more gentrified and arty streets of
> the new Marais is a sofa-packed lounge, the ideal place to collapse
> with magazines or a chess set. Paris' answer to the American Brunch
> Bar – fun, young, lively, cheapish – but not in the hectic Les Halles!
> Come for a brownie or a full-sized brunch selection of charcuteries,
> salads and pâtisseries. Waiters are frequently young foreign students,
> so no language problems. Not the place if you're in a hurry. People
> come here to relax over the papers and a café au lait. About 150f for
> brunch.

Café Beaubourg
(R)S   100 r. St Martin, 48 87 89 98, all cc (Hôtel de Ville)

> Unless breakfast is included in the hotel price, I usually prefer to wake
> myself up as the Parisians do – in bustling cafés. The quarter has as
> varied a selection of cafés as any, and the street corner next to the
> hotel satisfies me. But if you fancy the more trendy situation of a
> fashionable table in front of the Pompidou Centre then, with espresso
> machines gurgling and windows steaming, Café Beaubourg does a
> more extensive breakfast than most – fresh orange juice, eggs
> however you like them and a selection of breads and croissants with
> morning papers included for 70f.

Mariage Frères
(ST)M   30 bd. du Bourg Tibourg, 42 72 28 11, all cc, cl Mon, open 12 noon-5.30 pm
(Hôtel de Ville)

> However much the Brits may be mocked for their tea addiction,
> Parisians obviously like the stuff as well, judging by the range (nearly
> 400) available at this old-fashioned salon de thé. Waiters in white
> serve perfect pâtisseries on refined chinaware. Mozart tunes echo
> from behind the rows of tea and coffee crates. Only the prices (high
> for a tea room) recall the 1990s. Bank on 200f for a tummy-filling
> afternoon.

5th ARRONDISSEMENT

(Paris 75005)

The term Left Bank means more than simply the southern half of
Paris, and the 5th arrondissement is more than the famous Latin
Quarter. Following the banks of the Seine from the Jardin des Plantes
to the place St Michel, along the full length of the 'Boul Mich' (the
boulevard St Michel) to Porte Royale, the arrondissement has its own
very distinct quarters.

The Latin Quarter itself was first built upon by the Romans at the
same time that the Ile de la Cité was being colonised, but it was the
birth and development of the universities in the Middle Ages that gave
the area its name and character. The 13th-century Sorbonne is still at
the heart of the scholastic district. The streets of the quarter mostly

Shakespeare & Company

escaped the various grand designs that have shaped the boulevards of the rest of Paris, and it is still a place where students argue in cafés and cheap bookshops, and where midnight is no excuse to say goodnight. The important sites, such as the Panthéon – home of the remains of all those great Frenchmen who are not to be found in the cemetaries – on the top of the restaurant-dotted hill of St Geneviève; the Cluny museum and the Sorbonne itself are detailed in any tourist guide.

The true spirit of the quarter can be found in its love of the arts: the Théâtre de la Huchette, shoved between tourist-hustling restaurants, has Paris' longest running play, Ionesco's *The Bald Prima Donna*, the only production to compete with *The Mousetrap* for longevity; the scores of tiny cinemas – especially the essential Action chain – which show late night screenings of Cary Grant and Katherine Hepburn classics; and, most of all, Shakespeare & Company on the rue de la Bûcherie.

Here George Whitman, venerable patron saint of the young and inspired, presides over the world's most wonderful bookshop and sanctuary. Upstairs and down, new, second-hand and antiquarian books, all English language editions, are piled higgledy-piggledy in nooks and crannies. Between shelves, a rucksack may be stowed here, a blanket spread there, for penniless students and bibliophiles to sleep when the shop is closed. A couple of years ago a fire ravaged part of the tumbledown shop and destroyed much of the stock – but it did not touch the place's heart, wherein George Whitman's indomitable spirit still burns as truly as it has for the past several decades, a spirit encapsulated in the text above the door that reminds us not to be inhospitable to strangers, lest they be angels in disguise.

In the shadow of Notre Dame, across from the bookshop, is a contemporary church of the cathedral, the small 13th-century St Julien-le-Pauvre, where once were held student councils until tempers flew too high in the 16th century, and the church resumed concentration on religion rather than politics.

The rue Monge, home to a clairvoyant florist and other eccentric late night merchants, hides the remains of a 2nd-century Roman arena. The Arénes de Lutèce were only discovered a century ago and today form a local park. Here veterans play boules where once sport was played for higher stakes.

The rue Mouffetard, with its old-world twists and turns and new-world eateries, is popular with holidaying groups who believe they've found the true flavour of the left bank. They haven't. Hunt for restaurants in the quieter streets of the quarter Mouffetard.

Less literary than the rest of the quarter, the Mosque is worth a visit nonetheless, even if only for tea, and the Jardin des Plantes hosts the most central zoo in Paris.

Markets: pl. Maubert, Tue, Thurs, Sat (Maubert-Mutualité); pl. Monge, Wed, Fri, Sun (place Monge); bd. Port Royale, Tue, Thu, Sun (Port-Royale). All from 7 am-1.30 pm. Bouquinistes selling souvenirs on the river bank opposite Notre Dame.

HOTELS

➤ Le Jardin des Plantes
(H)M   5 r. Linné, 47 07 06 20, all cc (Jussieu)

> This is a true Entrée hotel. Although officially a mere two-star grading, this hotel can give many three- and four-star establishments a run for their money in the arrondissement. Nicely fitted rooms, decorated with a floral theme – each with a different flower – with little extras such as hair-driers, and communal treats such as the sauna and the rooftop rose garden for summer terrace breakfasts. Just opposite the Jardin des Plantes itself, the hotel is convenient for sightseeing. The ever helpful owners provide guests with English language notes on walks and sites in the area, and a pocket guide to the quarter. A welcome letter even gives a step-by-step guide to finding the hotel by public transport or car for the first time visitor to Paris. Nothing is too much trouble; if you need an iron and ironing board, just ask. Each return visit will bring something different – an art exhibition in the cellar, perhaps, or a musical evening. Double rooms with bath at just 550f – and even larger rooms on the top floor opening onto the roof garden cost just 640f. Arrowed for the welcome and facilities.

➤ Select Hotel
(H)L   1 pl. de la Sorbonne, 43 36 14 80, all cc (Luxembourg, St Michel, Sorbonne or Odéon)

> The Select's 19th century façade gives no clues to what lies inside. In 1988, owner M. Chabrérie decided to take the plunge with a complete revamp of the interior. Judging by the advance bookings he made the right choice. Inside is a hotch-potch of styles, materials and designs, combining old with new, marble and granite with leathers, fountains with beams. Over the top for some, but for many inspired and original. Nevertheless, the Select provides a relaxing haven from the outside bustle; soothing fountains gurgle in the hall, sumptuous leather armchairs are arranged in a series of small 'salons' surrounding the pretty garden. Downstairs is a spectacular vaulted cellar where an equally spectacular 30f buffet breakfast is served – excellent value for the array of fresh fruits, cereals, pâtisseries and juices on display. By night this is an intimate setting for cocktails and apéritifs. Rooms, all equipped with the usual gadgetry – TV, radio, hair-dryer, etc – range from 530f to 650f for a double. The welcome is warm, discreet and there when you want it. An arrow for the originality, location and comfort.

➤ Hôtel Esméralda
(H)M   4 r. St Julien le Pauvre, 43 54 19 20, no cc (St Michel)

> Next door to the improbably romantic bookshop, sanctuary and other-world known as Shakespeare and Company, the 'eccentric' utterly delightful Hotel Esméralda may not be everyone's cup of tea. It would be hard to find fault in the welcome, character and location

(overlooking Notre Dame on the edge of the Latin Quarter). The owner, Michelle Brunel, welcomes her guests like old friends; the hotel is furnished entirely to her whim – bohemian in keeping with the hotel's namesake, Victor Hugo's Esméralda, the gypsy heroine from *Notre Dame de Paris*. In every nook and cranny of this 15th-century house are souvenirs, *objets d'art*, ornaments akin to home more than hotel. Not recommended to sticklers for tidiness. Do check your room first – some are prone to early morning street noise, some have views of Notre Dame, some have no bathrooms. Breakfast is served in a panelled parlour decorated with paintings by the owner. Prices are excellent for the unique location – 370-420f for a double and 53f for breakfast. An arrow for the location and welcome.

Hôtel des Grandes Écoles
(H)M   *75 r. du Cardinal Lemoine, 43 26 79 23, V MC (Cardinal Lemoine or Monge)*

In such a touristy area, it's quite a surprise to find at the end of this pokey little alleyway three houses living in their own time warp. Undoubtedly the greatest attraction of the Grandes Ecoles hotel is its location, its garden and its peace and quiet. In summer months the gardens here are all flowers. Breakfast dining on the lawn is a rare pleasure in this part of the capital, with street noise lessened by surrounding plane trees. Inside is more eccentric and quaintly old-fashioned. The largest of the three houses has the reception area (try to get your room in this part if possible – it's the most recently done-up and, as a result, the most comfortable). Ask to see your room beforehand if taste (or lack of) and the occasional hint of wear and tear bothers you. Rooms in the annexe are a bit dull, drab and noisy and in need of a bit of love and attention – for lower budgets only. The welcome is not overly attentive and we were left to find our own way around. Prices range from around 500f for a double, 300f for a single with an uninspiring breakfast for 30f.

Sully St Germain
(H)L   *31 r. des Ecoles, 43 26 56 02, all cc (Maubert Mutualité)*

The sullen and unwelcoming weekend receptionist did not get my visit off to a good start. In fact at 800f a night for a three night stay, I was furious. But the rest of the staff were efficient and courteous – the lazy guy on duty that weekend cannot possibly stay for long. The hotel seems keen on improving its welcome: a sauna, jacuzzi and fitness centre are being fitted for 1993. To be honest, they will be needed to justify the room rates. Decor is what I term medieval – stone walls, fabric hangings and tapestries, not to mention a suit of armour. A confusing warren of basement rooms led to my accidentally having breakfast in the modern hotel next door. But then the Sully is a recent merger of two smaller hotels, with separate lifts in each wing. Do insist on a large bathroom, as some of the smaller ones have toilets designed to be ridden sidesaddle. All usual mod cons and freebies, shampoo, hair-drier and cable TV. I was sorely tempted to ditch this hotel from the guide, but its plans for 1993/4 look exciting enough for me to grant it a probational entry.

Résidence Henri IV

(H)L   50 r. des Bernadins, 44 41 31 81, V MC AE (Maubert Mutualité)

Opposite the tree-filled square Paul l'Angevin is this quiet hotel where your 750f pays for a charmingly finished room with more than just a mini-bar to store your purchases from the nearby boulevard St Germain street market. A small kitchenette in each of the 14 rooms allows one a little experimenting and adventure on an evening away from the restaurants. Cable TV.

RESTAURANTS

➔ Les Colonies

(R)M   10 r. St Julien le Pauvre, 43 54 31 33, V MC, dinner only, cl Sun (St Michel)

As the name implies, the theme and cuisine of this very comfortable little restaurant in the heart of the Latin Quarter are the colonies of France. Decor and food is a mixture of Asian and European cuisines. Decor is a vivid mix of silks, Chinese porcelains, drapes and soft lighting. Friendly waiters advise on the range of dishes available, all combining the exoticism of oriental food with the refinement of French cooking. An arrow for Les Colonies' originality in cuisine and decor. As we went to press the restaurant had a change of chef, and we agonised over keeping the arrow, but first reports of the new régime are very positive, with critics waxing lyrical over a rôti de chèvre à la muscade. Further comments welcomed. A menu at 170f is good value; otherwise budget around 300f.

➔ Le Coup Chou

(R)M   9-11 r. de Lanneau, 46 33 68 69, MC V (Maubert Mutualité)

For years I'd heard stories of this gloriously dotty and ivy-covered auberge-style restaurant tucked away in a timeless, touristless corner of the quarter. It takes some finding, as there appears to be no entrance to the restaurant. Eventually you will find your way in through a side door off the passageway of a private house in a nearby street (the impasse Charretière)! Messieurs Nani, Lemonnier and Azzopardi create a delightful menu that is no more straightforward. Even the canny and loyal regulars have to ask for elucidation of the mouthwatering suggestions such as magret de canard, cooked with peaches or the salmon fillet marinated in lime juice. The welcome is of the warmest, and the table appointments refreshingly simple: brass candlesticks and functional cruet on plain white linen. At 300f the set carte-menu is not the cheapest, but is never dull. Arrowed for individual charm.

L'Epoque
(R)S   81 r. du Cardinal Lemoine, 46 34 15 84, MC V (+150f), cl Sun (Cardinal Lemoine)

A 60f menu served in the evening. All praise to Pascal and Xavier for creating a down-to-earth restaurant in the oh-so-popular Mouffetard quarter. Just yards away the rue Mouffetard itself lures tourists into its countless restaurants and bistros, but here, away from the crush of American Express cardholders, the locals repair for a nourishing meal with friends. Xavier holds court in the simple but homely dining room, whilst his partner busies himself in the kitchen preparing food bought twice a day from the local markets. The entrées, such as the warm herring salad or my fish terrine (which guarded the texture and flavour of each of its ingredients) are sensible and reliable. Main courses, however, are not for those who wish to avoid meat – my truite meunière was rather dry. It's the confit de canard and solid beef-style fare that keeps the customers happy. The place is cheery and warmhearted and neither an English nor American voice within earshot.

Le Petit Prince
(R)SM   12 r. de Lanneau, 43 54 77 26, M V AE, cl lunch (Maubert Mutualité)

Gilles Gobe and Armand Floux run a laid back and reliable late night eatery. Standard classic fare neither disappoints nor surprises – duck and veal standards and quenelles sauce dieppoise for example. Menus at 82f for two courses and 140f for three are served and enjoyed at leisure. Unusual not to be hassled out of a restaurant in the fifth (if spending less than 100f a head) and allowed to enjoy an evening.

Sud Ouest
(R)SM   ^0 r. Montagne Ste Geneviève, 46 33 30 46, all cc, cl Sun, Aug (Maubert Mutualité)

In a street boasting an eclectic array of specialities from raclette to sushi comes this (mostly) cellar restaurant offering the tastes of south-western France. The decor almost parodies an Aquitaine cave, and the result is an eccentric collection of wine bottles, staircases and tables in every nook and cranny. Plastic ivy plummets down a genuine centuries-old well and bottles of Bordeaux rest in sabots and every other hiding place imaginable. Apparently the place was once a crypt but the regional cuisine is alive and well. The usual selection – salad of foie gras and the ubiquitous magret; but other specialities, a chilled tomato soup with basil and a seasonal cassoulette of cèpes and girolles, are worth a look. A savoury finish to the meal comes with a heady papillote of chèvre à l'Armagnac – pity that the accompanying green salad is so sparse. A la carte hits the 300f mark, and there are two menus at 125f and 190f. The wine list is short and to the point – south-westerners from the Tarn, Cahors, Bergerac and Bordeaux regions, but there are 5 Champagnes and 3 Burgundies!

La Timonerie
(R)M   *35 q. de la Tournelle, 43 25 44 42, MC V, cl Sun, Mon (Maubert Mutualité)*

The quai de la Tournelle is where the serious eating occurs in the 5th. Greek restaurants and fake bistros may do good business around the metro stations, but on this quiet stretch of the Seine, facing the Ile St Louis, restaurants serve gourmets. La Tour d'Argent boasts more than a view – it is universally acclaimed as *the* table of Paris, with its incomparable views and legendary cuisine. The Michelin and Gault et Millau already do it justice, but this Entrée is not generally concerned with 1,000f à la carte dinners – even if one can lunch for around 400f (wine not included) on weekdays. Instead, take a stroll along the quayside to see what else can inspire the serious foodie. Philippe de Givency reigns at La Timonerie, and comes up with little gems such as the petatou poitevin, which turns out to be a moreish tartelette of potato and goat's cheese with a chive cream sauce. Pork marinated with cumin was another temptation on the September menu. But each month brings its own delights in this light ground-floor dining room. Lunch menu is 195f, otherwise pay 400f.

Clavel
(R)SM   *65 q. de la Tournelle, 46 33 18 65, V MC, cl Sun, Mon, Aug (Maubert Mutualité)*

Don't be put off by the anonymous chrome and venetians style of the restaurant. The chef Jean-Yves Guichard is a man to be trusted with coquilles St Jacques and ravioli de homard breton style. A full dinner could set you back 400f, but at lunchtimes the 160f menu is one of the catches of the quai.

Le Bistrot du Port
(R)M   *13 q. de Montibello, 40 51 73 19, MC V, cl Mon, Tue lunch (St Michel)*

Pay 155f for the set menu and have a passable dinner served by attentive and welcoming staff in this theatrical, colonial-style restaurant on the popular stretch of the quais. The welcome is as warm for a large group of friends as for a loving couple in the smallish dining room.

Le Saint Hilaire
(B)S   *2 r. Valette, 46 33 52 42 (Maubert Mutualité)*

If you've over-indulged at lunchtime, but fancy a late night snack, then this bar with its billiards, beers and boisterous conversation offers a choice of moules, moules or moules. Mussels any way you want them (marinières, gratinées, with escargots) served with a plate of frites and glass of Alsatian beer – all for 50f. Open from early morning until 2 am.

Atelier de Maître Albert
(R)M   1 r. Maître Albert, 73 q. de la Tournelle, 46 33 13 78, all cc, cl Sun, open for dinner only (Cité or St Michel)

> Squeezed in between an unnavigable maze of Latin Quarter backstreets is this classic Parisian auberge where Cyrano de Bergerac would have felt at home – old oak beams, vast open fireplaces and roaring log fires with the odd addition of discreet lighting to boost the candlelight. Although he might have raised an eyebrow at the swing seats at the bar. The food is as attractive as the surroundings. A 250f menu bought succulent fish quenelles, magret de canard and a delectable crème brulée accompanied by a half bottle of wine (Bordeaux or Sauvignon); each course has a choice of five dishes. Service is attentive without overdoing it, leaving you to enjoy soothing classical background music.

Perraudin
(R)S   157 r. St Jacques, 46 33 15 75, cl Sat lunch, Sun pm and Aug (Luxembourg)

> One of my favourites in the Sorbonne/Latin Quarter area for a quick snack or meal on the cheap. The Gloaguen family have made it their business to preserve good, old-fashioned French cooking. And they've succeeded, judging by this little restaurant's popularity. Thick French onion soup, boeuf bourguignon, escargots served plain and simple, crème caramel – all the old favourites found in recipe books but rarely in restaurants. To attract the young (usually Sorbonne students) as well as the old (Sorbonne professors) Perraudin has introduced a Sunday brunch menu – andouillette served in a mustard sauce, scrambled eggs the French way, and naturally Bloody Marys. The wine list has an interesting selection of unknown, frequently underestimated wines served by the pitcher or glassful. The 60f lunch menu is limited but interesting – otherwise bank on 100f a head.

Rue de la Huchette
(R)S   (St Michel)

> This street, and its tributaries, is not so much the Latin quarter as the Greek quarter. Scores of restaurateurs stand in doorways, holding out plates of kebabs, taramasalata, salad and stuffed peppers, as they courteously hustle punters from the pavement into the restaurant. Generally though, once inside, attention is not quite so intense, and diners are left to enjoy the meal relatively hassle free. At the Auberge Crétoise du Minotaure I had a three-course lunch for 58f. Impossible to select one of the charcoal-burning tavernas above the others – wander around, stand firm and choose.

Café de la Mosque de Paris
(ST)S   39 r. Geoffroy-St Hilaire, 43 31 18 14, no cc (Censier Daubenton)

> A quiet haven in another continent behind the Jardin des Plantes, the Paris Mosque serves green mint tea to calm the stressed visitor.

6th ARRONDISSEMENT

(Paris 75006)

With the boulevard St Michel to one side and the rue des Sèvres on the other, the 6th arrondissement spreads from the Seine almost as far as the Montparnasse tower and is the most bustling and commercial of the three districts lining the left bank.

The Luxembourg is the luxury park within the quarter but the real heart is the boulevard St Germain that bisects the arrondissement. From here spread the streets of 'typical left bank hotels' that have filled the honeymoon scrapbooks of Boston and Wisconsin, Guildford and Edinburgh. Sadly, many of the commercial establishments of the three left bank areas trade on the city's reputation and past, rather than pay attention to the present. There are exceptions, and many of them are listed in the Entrée.

First impressions matter a great deal, and most of us discover the quarter from the place St Michel. Noisy, boisterous with a hint of celebration about it, this is a more exciting starting point than the boulevard St Germain where you will inevitably find yourself, as any road that does not lead to the Seine disgorges on the big boulevard itself. So take the old and winding rue St André des Arts with its even smaller tributaries such as the passage de l'Hirondelle and the rue Gît-le-Coeur. Restaurants, cafés, hotels and galleries line the narrow street. Here stood the first guillotines, here lodged musketeers, here is the Paris that the cinema promised us.

The end of the St André has food stalls during the morning in the bustling rue Buci, and croissants throughout the night at the 24-hour boulangerie in the rue de l'Ancienne Comédie. There is a Drugstore at St Germain, with a bar specialising in countless varieties of bottled beer from all over Europe, and record and book departments open until the small hours for late night shopping sprees.

At the place St Germain-des-Prés buskers and street-performers entertain the crowds who have come in search of the great existentialists (see listings below).

The Odéon is the home of one of Paris' most important theatres, which stands in a charming square, the left bank home of the classics for those who do not fancy crossing the river to the Comédie Française.

But cross the river do, even if only halfway, to spend a romantic moment on the wooden footbridge Pont des Arts. At night it justifies the description City of Lights, and at sunrise Paris has never looked lovelier.

Markets: bd. Raspail, Tue, Fri (Rennes) 7 am-1.30 pm; covered market, St Germain 3 ter r. Mabillon (Mabillon) Tue-Sat 8 am-1 pm, 4-7.30 pm, Sun 8 am-1 pm. Bouquinistes line the quais of the Seine.

Festival: Foire St Germain, June-July – poetry and music.

Le Voltaire

HOTELS

Hôtel Lutetia
(H)L   *42 bd. Raspail, 49 54 46 46, all cc (Sèvres-Babylone)*

It was ten years since last I stayed at the Lutetia, and my memories were of draughty, dowdy corridors and rattling radiators in a seedy, faded barn of a hotel, so the renaissance of the only Grand Hotel on the Rive Gauche is more than welcome. Tattinger's young and dynamic management team have enthusiastically overseen the resurrection which is by no means finished. And it's the ongoing nature of the renovation that adds to the charm. The reception and main salons are splendid in their red plush glory, but the long passages upstairs are reassuringly in need of attention – happily as dingy as ever. One by one the bedrooms have been refitted and redesigned. Styles vary: some are equipped with authentic furniture from 1910, others more conventionally turned out. The jewel of the hotel's 300 bedrooms is the honeymoon suite, which is surely the ultimate lovers' hideaway for those whose Parisian dreams were inspired by Gene Kelly and Hollywood. Through the salon, past the gloriously light and spacious bathroom with its odd and mismatched windows, and up the wooden staircase to the bedroom itself. An eyrie nook high above the hotel's famous neon sign, is thrust into the Paris skyline. The view from the stone cave of a balcony is perfect, from Montmartre to Montparnasse and, in the centre, the Eiffel Tower itself. Thankfully the Lutetia remains more Rive Gauche than Grand Hotel. The red drapes of the salon and bar are expensive enough a background for the hotel's neighbour and *habituée* Catherine Deneuve, often seen holding court with the scribblers from *Madame Figaro* and *Elle*. For the locals the Lutetia, like the Bon Marché department store across the road, is the essential heart of the quarter. The Gastronomique restaurant, Le Paris and the bustling Brasserie Lutetia (ditto) are the essential meeting-places whether for the dreaded business breakfast or the intimate celebration. Guests' breakfast in the Salon Borghese, serenaded over Sunday brunch by musicians in the minstrels' gallery.

➔ Relais Saint Germain
(H)L   *9 Carrefour de l'Odéon, 43 29 12 05, all cc (Odéon)*

For many, judging by the advance bookings, this is the perfect hotel – no pretensions, no eccentric decor, no over- or under-attentive staff. The Relais Saint Germain epitomises that rare breed of hotel where all is professional, yet discreet, luxurious without being over the top, all thanks to M. Laipsker the owner. Ordinary from the outside, but beyond the porch is a museum's worth of beautiful paintings, antiques and luxuriant plants. Rooms are well-sized with well-tended houseplants, fresh flowers and yet more paintings. I'd come for the breakfast alone – how refreshing to find more than just a croissant and pre-packed jam with your café au lait. Included in the room price is a breakfast feast of breads, freshly squeezed juices, cereals, yogurts and fruit salads. Prices, as to be expected in a hotel of this quality and location, are high – 1,400f for a double. Worthwhile for splurges.

Hôtel Ferrandi
(H)M   *92 r. du Cherche Midi, 42 22 97 40 (St Placide or Sèvres-Babylone)*

More home than hotel with comfy furniture, roaring fire, family photos; decor perhaps not to everyone's taste, but the real bonus here is the owner, Madame Lafond, who welcomes her guests like long lost friends. Rooms are large, well-equipped and mostly blue (clearly Madame's favourite colour). Prices not excessive for relative luxury and excellent location close to St Germain in a street lined with antique shops, old boutiques and interesting façades. Double rooms go for anything between 385f and 880f with breakfast an overpriced 50f. If the Ferrandi is full, Madame will surely point you in the direction of her second establishment – the (arrowed) Hôtel de l'Elysée in the 8th arrondissement.

Relais Christine
(H)L   *3 r. Christine, 43 26 71 80, all cc, valet parking*

Once upon a time this was a convent – today it is a peaceful haven in a bustling quarter. All rooms are different in size and decor, but share an elegance, from the fabrics to the pink Portuguese marble bathrooms. Tranquillity comes best in a room looking out onto the courtyard – but at a price. The 34 bedrooms cost between 1,100-1,500f.

➤Hôtel St Paul
(H)M   *43 r. Monsieur le Prince, 43 26 98 64, all cc (Odéon)*

Detective Sergeant Hawkins, late of Scotland Yard, fell in love with Paris when seconded to Interpol some twenty years ago. So he opened a hotel – right next door to the Polidor restaurant. Originally just one-star, it has blossomed into a meticulously run three-star establishment. The French love the place – perhaps it is the charming decor, the pocket handkerchief garden that lures a bright variety of butterflies and birds into the funnel of a courtyard, or Mr Hawkins's eccentric hobby of growing tomato plants in the hotel window boxes. Bedrooms on lower floors are tall and stately. Room rates vary from 450-820f for two. Breakfast at 40f is served in the old cellar which boasts its original old stone well. Arrowed for attention to detail.

St André des Arts
(H)M   *66 r. St André, 43 26 96 16, no cc (Odéon)*

One time residence of the royal musketeers, odd quirks of decor and furnishings throw back to the days of fiction and romance: pew seats, little low doors, and the quaint toilet between the first and second floors. Rooms at 300-400f are pleasingly furnished, but nothing is in the luxury class. Nonetheless, the atmosphere of the place and the informal and helpful staff keep a loyal clientele, even amongst the beautiful people who could afford something far more sleek and chic. Sunday morning's breakfast is a muted cavalcade of bright young things coping with the effects of Saturday night.

Quality Inn Rive Gauche
(H)M   *92 r. Vaugirard, 42 22 00 56, all cc, open all night (St Placide)*

The Entrée does not normally feature chain hotels, and this conventional three-star tourist establishment might not have found its way into these pages, but for its seventh floor. Here all the rooms are named after great French writers and artists. The dressing tables contain examples of the manuscript from letters and diaries of Stendhal, Hugo, Rousseau, Voltaire or whoever is inscribed on the door. Baths have whirlpool spa attachments and the euphemistic tea and coffee-making facilities (hotel-speak for kettle) is amongst the extras provided. Several rooms have been adapted for wheelchair access.

→**Hôtel St Michel**
(H)S   *17 r. Gît-le-Coeur, 43 26 98 70, no cc (St Michel)*

Proof that modesty can triumph over pretention and win one of our arrows for value and service in the process, comes in an improbable haven of tranquillity at the heart of bustling St Michel. Tucked away behind the metro and thronging pavements of the place St Michel is the quaintly named rue Gît-le-Coeur, as convenient for the right bank as the left. Twixt the hustle and the Seine, halfway down the road is this one-star hotel kept spotlessly clean by M. et Mme Mécelle. Guests are greeted by the pot pourrl at the foot of the stairs, and in the tiny reception area is a little bookcase with Agatha Christie and Enid Blyton paperbacks in both French and English. Useful in a hotel that shuts its front door at 1 am sharp. Rooms range from the modest one-bedroomed 22, at 195f, to the mini-suite number 14 at just 390f. Breakfast is included in the room rate, and is taken in an excavated 'cave' at the foot of the pretty, tiled staircase. The original centuries-old spiral staircase conceals a pretty washroom. The hotel has no lift.

Belloy St Germain
(H)L   *2 r. Racine, 46 34 26 50, no cc (St Michel)*

Jean Philippe Lattron has modernised the old one-star St Michel lodging house to the present three-star hotel, with plenty of mirrors and plush, efficient decor. Two lifts and the mod cons expected at 820f per night.

La Louisiane
(H)M   *60 r. de Seine, 43 29 59 30, all cc (Mabillon)*

Simone de Beauvoir, Amanda Lear, Jean-Paul Sartre all stayed here, but not recently. The one-time guest list keeps this hotel in many of the traditional guide books. That and the fact that the rooms overlook the bustling rue Bucci street market with its tantalising morning smells. But I am afraid that it rather trades on its reputation, despite a renovation programme that may mean that rooms on the top floor might actually be served by the lift. The atmosphere and welcome was at best sterile. Rooms adequately furnished. Breakfast is a dull affair, self-service with sliced bread and pour your own juice/coffee points in a dreary room on the 3rd floor. Considering the all-night croissant shop, the Boulangerie de l'Ancienne Comédie is just around the corner, you'd do best to make your own arrangements. No better than a convenient place to sleep. Not cheap.

L'Hôtel
(H)L   *13 r. des Beaux Arts, 43 25 27 22, all cc (St Germain-des-Près)*

Here Oscar Wilde 'died beyond his means', but in those days it was called the Hôtel d'Alsace. Today's visitors might follow in his example if unaware of the room rates. More than 2,000f for the very room itself, or perhaps the oval boudoir fitted with Mistinguettes, exotic bedroom furnishings. Once a pavillon d'amour, the building was extended in the last century to become a 6-storey hotel. The street has always attracted the great and the good. Mérimée Pradier and Corot were amongst the former residents. In 1968 the hotel was reconstructed and today Guy-Louis Duboucheron's guests, paying around 1,000f per night, can enjoy a fine restaurant, comfortable salons, and imposing luxury.

RESTAURANTS

Polidor
(R)S   *41 r. Monsieur le Prince, 43 26 95 34, no cc (Odéon)*

The Polidor is a deep brown memory of a lunchtime. A triumph of genuine atmosphere over gastronomy. The 50f two-course weekday lunch menu is a favourite of the mixed clientele: locals, businessmen on a budget and cost-conscious students. Evenings and weekends offer three courses for 100f. But à la carte for two can still see change from a 200f note – and that includes wine by the way. The quality of food varies. Truite meunière was fine, poulet basque bland, sorbet over-sugary, but chocolate tart scrummy. Candid waitresses warn clients off the kitchen's less successful efforts, so do listen. And check the specials scrawled on mirrors and blackboards around the period dining room. Guests share long tables designed for six or sixteen in the noisy and cheery front room. The tiled floor and pretty painted walls of the back room might suit less sociable diners.

Bistrot de la Grille
(R)M   *14 r. Mabillon, 43 54 16 87, MC V (St Sulpice)*

Smothered with pictures of classic film stars (save the smattering roll call of French presidents behind the bar), the tiny restaurant continues its picture theme on its menus, each bound with stills from a different classic movie. Mine was Gigi, a friend was served with a Fernandel favourite. If you are staying in the quarter, this is the place, not for your gastronomic treat, but for a long evening's lazy chat and eavesdropping in a bustling left bank bistro. It is always packed, so be prepared to spend 15 minutes propping up the bar before eating. You cannot eat à la carte, and the menu is 140f. Entrées are dull in the extreme – unimaginative fare, garnished with a lettuce leaf. But main courses offer more satisfaction. Take a tip from the film photos, and stick to the classics. Pot au feu or the ragout of duck with olives, served in the copper. Same advice for desserts. Crème brulée and prunes recommended. In one of the least touristy side streets of this popular quarter, the bistro has been a local choice for ages. My last visit was slightly worrying, a 10% hike in prices, and the cheery service seemed more slapdash than usual. Whether this is indicative of a decline, I know not yet. It may simply have been part of the city's August malaise. I've asked chums in the quarter to keep an eye on the place.

La Méditerranée
(R)L   *2 pl. de l'Odéon, 43 26 46 75, all cc (Odéon)*

'Thanks to La Méditerranée, the sea has arrived at the Place de l'Odéon,' wrote Jean Cocteau in 1960 and his penmanship and sketching adorns the menus and plates of this favourite haunt of the actors, directors and politicians who frequent the national theatre opposite. The decor throughout the restaurant is original work of artists and stage designers of the 20th century, the Belloni ceiling of the inner room much admired. There are menus at 215 and 300f. A la carte dinner should come to 700-800f. The menu changes three times a year, but eternal favourites are the house bouillabaisse and the legendary bar grille fenouil au jus. Nothing is ever pre-cooked or frozen, and the chef refuses to buy second rate, so have a second choice ready should your menu selection be unavailable. Service is unhurried under the direction of Laurence Bouquet.

La Fourchette en Habit
(R)S   *75 r. du Cherche Midi, 45 48 82 74, MC V, cl Sat lunch and all day Mon (Sèvres-Babylone)*

What would the 6th arrondissement be without its wonderful rue du Cherche Midi. In fact at midday the road is chock-a-block with Renaults desperately seeking a parking place before playing hunt the table. The choice of restaurants is enviable, and a short break in Paris could be gastronomically fulfilled without ever leaving the street. A favourite with locals looking for simple sustenance is La Fourchette. Its exclusively fishy menu is mainly traditional in style. Serviceable seafood platters are a speciality. The decor is pink and picturesque, with mirrored murals of bathing beauties. The two tables on the pavement are sought after in summer. You can pay around 150f or, as we did, choose the 85f lunch menu, finding a workmanlike fish soup and acceptable sole in olive oil.

➤ Joséphine, 'Chez Dumonet'
(R)L   *117 r. du Cherche Midi, 45 48 52 40, MC V (Sèvres-Babylone)*

Closed Saturday, Sunday and July, but next door's rôtisserie (which shares the same kitchen) is open during those periods. Those in the know visit Joséphine on Wednesday, because that is when they serve the legendary gigot d'agneau. Lamb comes in many varieties on the menu proper, but the gigot, served with its Vendean dish of beans is exclusive to Wednesdays. You will pay more than 250f for your meal, but even a glance at the wonderful wine list tells you that this is no run of the mill bistro. For many this is the jewel of the indispensible Cherche Midi. Arrowed for Wednesday.

La Marlotte
(R)M   *55 r. du Cherche Midi, 45 48 86 79, all cc (Sèvres-Babylone)*

Don't be put off by the unimaginative plastic decor. Lucie and Michel's eatery, halfway down the Cherche Midi, is one of the best places in the street. One speciality – liver served in a raspberry vinegar – has been luring one local resident through the door ever since she moved to the quarter two years ago. Pay under 200f for dinner.

Chez Marie
(R)M   *25 r. Servandoni, 46 33 12 06, cl Aug, Sat lunch and all Sunday (St Sulpice)*

As could be expected from a restaurant located right next to the Senate, all here is reliable, staid and efficient – no surprises, no disasters. Clientele are sober-faced businessmen and supportive friends of Marie herself. No intruding noises, no loud music, no eccentric decor to distract, just still lives and portraits on plain walls. Little has changed here over the years other than a few extra tables to cope with demand. Even prices have varied little from the current 250-300f for a substantial three-courser. No major gastronomic surprises either, just good, classical French cuisine. Friend dined on coquilles Saint Jacques served with a light mousseline of watercress – a clear success. Likewise a boeuf bourguignon – succulent and unmessed about. Iced hazelnut mousse followed – light and delicious.

A la Cour de Rohan
(ST)M   *59-61 r. St André des Arts, 43 25 79 67, no cc, cl Mon, August; open 12 noon-7 pm Tues-Fri, 3-11.30 pm Sat, 3-7 pm Sun (Odéon)*

A la Cour de Rohan verges on the cosy English tea parlour where ladies sip with fingers crooked, discussing art exhibitions in hushed tones. Elegant, refined, just the occasional clink of china to interrupt the gentle background classical music; not a crumb or pastry fork out of place. Prices not the lowest – 60f for tea or sumptuous hot chocolate with the freshest of home-made tartes.

La Cabanne d'Auvergne
(R)S   *44 r. Grégoire des Tours, 43 25 14 75, no cc, cl Sun and Mon lunch (Odéon or Mabillon)*

After a half-hour search for La Cabanne (beware – boulevard St Germain cuts through rue Grégoire des Tours – no. 44 is on the northern side) we could have come to no better place to satisfy our by then much-grown appetites. Students, budgeters and the hungry come to eat, drink and enjoy, Auvergne-style. The owner meets and greets in auvergnat shirt complete with black beret; milking stools, country casseroles and copper pots hang from the ceiling; tables are wooden and scrubbed. Not good for intimate evenings. By the end of the evening, everyone is sharing tables and, if you get on well enough, food and wine. Portions are colossal; few have made it through the 'assiette de charcuterie', especially if preceded by rich auvergnat cheese soup; a potée auvergnate (Auvergne's version of the hot-pot) proved the perfect winter warmer. Around 150f for more than you can cope with. Good home-grown wines from 70f.

Petit Saint Benoît

(R)S   4 r. St Benoît, 42 60 27 92, no cc, cl Sat and Sun, open 12 noon-2.30 pm and 7-10 pm (St-Germain-des-Près)

The archetypal Parisian café this – and has been for 130 years. Regulars return again and again for the same old menu, the same dish, served by the same waitress. Food is standard café/brasserie grub – sauté de veau, tarte aux fruits, nothing exciting, just good, cheap (100f for a good lunch) and unpretentious.

Les Deux Magots

(B)   6 pl. St-Germain-des-Près, 45 48 55 25 (St-Germain-des-Près)

They come in search of Hemingway and Sartre, and find others who have come in search of Hemingway and Sartre. Homage is paid with a role of Kodak and a coffee at the 'very tables … '. Tourists flock here all year – as well as to the Café de Flore next door. Even the Parisian intellectuals who hang around this former haunt of the existentialists and surrealists, come to this chic café to see, be seen, to hear and be heard. Non-French speakers risk feeling left out of the action. But its location, right on place de Saint-Germain-des-Près warrants a visit. Food is standard café snacks.

Café de Flore

(B)   172 bd. St-Germain, 45 48 55 26 (St-Germain-des-Près)

The other left bank café where tourists watch other tourists and street performers.

La Coupole

(R)SM   102 bd. Montparnasse, 43 20 14 20, all cc (Vavin)

The most famous brasserie in all Paris is now part of the Flo family. Seafood a speciality (witness the enormous selection on display outside) with all the standard dishes available. Eat well for 250f.

Le Procope

(R)SM   13 r. de l'Ancienne Comédie, 43 26 99 20, AE MC V, until 2 am (St-Germain-des-Près)

Three centuries worth of celebrities have flocked to Le Procope – Rousseau, Hugo, Balzac, Robespierre … Voltaire even left his desk behind for all to admire. Nowadays it is tourists who flock here, frequently outnumbering the Parisians. Recommended therefore to non-French speakers (English the common language) and historians, rather than the gastronome. Food is mediocre – at least 100f for a substantial lunch and more than double that for the dinner menu. Shellfish recommended.

7th ARRONDISSEMENT

(Paris 75007)

The least familiar of the left bank trinity, the 7th arrondissement takes in an enormous sweep of the Seine between two of Paris' most celebrated attractions, the Musée d'Orsay and the Eiffel Tower, and forms a wedge inland as far as Unesco's building, a stone's throw from Montparnasse.

As to Gustave Eiffel's tower, we have radio to thank for its continued appearance in posters, postcards and Ealing comedies. The controversial structure, erected in 1889, was built as a rather natty flagpole for the centenary of the Revolution. It certainly was not expected to last another 100 years.

However, after Marconi and his followers made their contributions to the field of communications a large mast was required – and so the luxuriously latticed ironwork in the Champ de Mars was spared to the bicentennial and beyond.

The Gare d'Orsay opened to a fanfare on Bastille Day 1900, the gateway for the railways of the 20th century to south-western France. Within four decades it had closed, and from 1939 this magnificent building languished by the river, serving as temporary auction house, prisoner reception centre, and even film location. In 1977 President Giscard d'Estaing decided that the Gare should live again, decreeing that it would become a museum of 19th century art. Six years later, his successor, François Mitterand, declared the Musée d'Orsay the link between the art treasures of the Louvre and the modern works of the Pompidou Centre.

The magnificent building itself is worth a visit – quite apart from the priceless collection of Impressionist and early Symbolist paintings housed within.

The Musée Rodin is also to be found in the quarter, and some stunning hôtels particuliers, should you be fortunate enough to peek through an open doorway. The essential department store for Parisians (rather than the Galeries Lafayette and Printemps which essentially market themselves to visitors) is Au Bon Marché, designed by Gustave Eiffel, on the corner of the rue des Sèvres and the rue du Bac.

On sunny summer Sunday mornings a rainbow is guaranteed, courtesy of the city's fire department. The young pompier cadets are given lessons on directing their power hoses on the river bank below the quai Voltaire. The water sprays create a romantic link across the river from the Orsay to the Louvre. Excellent views from the bridges.

Hedonism is served at the Piscine Déligny, where perfect tans and improbable waistlines are flaunted on the decks of the floating pool on the Seine.

Market: Saxe-Breteuil, av. de Saxe, Thu, Sat (Sèvres-Lecourbe) 7 am-1.30 pm.

Hôtel Duc de Saint Simon

HOTELS

➤ Duc de St Simon

(H)L   *14 r. St Simon, 45 48 35 66, no cc (rue du Bac)*

Just step into the 200-year-old courtyard with its climbing wisteria and geranium pots, and you are transported into another world of tranquillity and quality. You'd never believe this was once a humble family pension. Those with the money to spend on a grand international palace hotel come here if they have managed to retain the taste for the genuinely good things in life. This is the grande luxe of a country manor house, in the city. Rooms, which do not come cheap at between 1,000 and 2,000f, are the nearest thing to perfection that you'll find at the price. Positively creaking with antiques, they have a very particular charm, one that is carried through into the trompe l'oeil public rooms, especially the lovely bar and lounge converted from the old stone cellars. Many rooms look out onto the lush gardens which are closed to guests. Others have rooftop terraces. No credit cards accepted here, but Eurocheques and Travellers Cheques taken. Breakfast is 70f. The arrow is for the stylish retreat and charming welcome – not the prices.

➤ Nevers

(H)M   *83 r. du Bac, 45 44 61 30, no cc (rue du Bac)*

This converted annexe to an adjacent convent is the domaine of Mme Ireland. Rooms have flourishing windowboxes and each of the 11 bedrooms is named after a different flower. On the first three floors there are only two rooms to a landing. The hotel has no lift, so only the fit will benefit from the ever-popular top floor. Room 11 is the cherished secret of many regulars who adore its tiny, yet completely secluded rooftop terrace for private sunbathing or romantic breakfasts. Rooms are well fitted, with good bathrooms, mini-bar, but no TV. The nightly rate is a good value 390f with shower or 400f with bath. Arrowed for value and welcome.

Solférino

(H)M   *91 r. de Lille, 47 05 85 54, V MC (Assemblée Nationale)*

I like the top floor bedrooms under the eaves in this hotel behind the Musée d'Orsay. Take the lift to the fourth floor and climb the extra flight of stairs to the servants' quarters. Sweet, prettily decorated bedrooms with tiny bathrooms hidden in cupboards. Room rates around the 500f mark include the cost of breakfast which may be served in the rooms, but should really be taken in the very attractive little morning room decorated with a collection of plates and porcelain. A very nice little hotel that retains its charm despite its popularity. Advance booking advisable.

Bersolys St Germain
(H)M   *28 r. de Lille, 42 60 73 79, MC V (rue du Bac)*

> At 600f a night the hotel has all the usual electrical extras, TV, hair-dryer etc, and the added bonus of antiques in some of the rooms, which reflect the shop windows of the antiquaires along the road.

Quai Voltaire
(H)M   *19 q. Voltaire, 42 61 50 91, all cc (rue du Bac)*

> Popular for the views across the Seine, and convenient for the Musée d'Orsay along the road, this 600f a night hotel has always boasted an international clientele – Sibelius, Wagner and Wilde amongst those whose autograph may be viewed in the slightly garish salon. Rooms are pleasantly furnished, but upstaged by the stunningly floodlit Louvre opposite.

RESTAURANTS

➤ Le Divellec
(R)L   *107 r. de l'Université, 45 51 91 96, all cc, cl Sun, Mon, Aug (Invalides)*

> Jacques le Divellec knows his onions, and shallots, but more than that this ex-pat Breton knows his oysters. And when there's a pearl in the month the good, the great and the nostalgic mariners head to the quartier des Invalides. The leaders of France have shaped Europe's destiny pampered by a seafood supper prepared by the acknowledged captain of the seas. Divellec has braved the deep as a trawlerman, and his instinct for quality rarely fails him. A range of oysters to impress the most critical diner is matched by an audacity that never fails to intrigue. Who else would serve foie gras with St Jacques? Friends, on tasting the experiment, called me up to insist on Divellec's entry in this Entrée. A usually flat sole levitated to glory via an hollandaise that wafted the heady scent of Pouilly Fuisse. And on dry land, desserts are equally heroic. Fixed price menus start around the 300f mark, and à la carte will cost in the region of 500f.

La Fontaine de Mars
(R)S   *129 r. St Dominique, 47 05 46 44, V MC (Ecole Militaire)*

> The row of neat polished copper pans on the wall states that this is a good old-fashioned restaurant. The row of neat cropped hairstyles at the tables states that the place has been discovered by the fashionable young things of the district. Never mind, this is the gingham-draped café-restaurant of your Maigret-monochrome-tinted memories, where

souvenirs of simple French meals around the country are inspired by the reliable cuisine. Boudin aux pommes, a succulent pork terrine and mouthwatering oeufs en meurette are good for starters. The house speciality is a fricassée de canard. Pay just 85f for the lunchtime menu – and even à la carte will keep you on the safe side of 200f. A good workaday wine list has some reliable bottles from 60f.

Thoumieux
(R)S   79 r. St Dominique, 47 05 49 75, no cc (Invalides)

The chic meet the cheap, as the two identities of the district merge in one enormous bistro. Fashionable couples squeeze past cash-crisis students to enjoy the dishes on this wide-ranging menu. The cassoulet may not be the greatest this side of Toulouse, but the predominantly southern fare is none the less tasty and nourishing. Best of all, according to the two regulars who introduced me to the place, is the tête du veau. Where else can you eat this well at this price? they asked – this price being anything from the remarkably good 52f menu to the à la carte boat-pushing-out total of around 150f. A no-nonsense wine list with bargains from the 50f mark helps keep costs down and excuses the excruciating pun in the restaurant's name.

Le Télégraphe
(R)SM   41 r. de Lille, 40 15 06 65, AE MC V (rue du Bac)

A gloriously cool and spacious restaurant with improbably high ceiling has the air of an operatic interpretation of a 19th-century European railway station – a fitting lunch venue after a morning's culture infusion at the grande gare itself, the Musée d'Orsay. Don't expect a gastronomic revelation, but be satisfied with modestly successful standards. Have a pleasant piments aux courgettes et piments doux or go for the salmony standards. Menus are 125f at lunchtime and 175f all day. A la carte will cost at least double that. In nice weather sit outside on the garden terrace.

Chez Germaine
(R)S   30 r. Pierre Leroux, 42 73 28 34, no cc (Vanneau)

You don't need paper money here. A pocket full of loose change will feed you in the bargain of the student district. Not just students, but the older inhabitants of the quarter queue on the pavements – the place is full by 1 pm – to lunch chez Germaine. Well, with a full menu – including wine – at 60f can you blame them. A la carte comes to around 45f for two courses, 80f for the whole hog. Hog is just about the only thing not on the extensive carte of basic standards. My companion had three doorstep wedges of pink cold roast beef served with a heavy dollop of potato salad. My quenelles of brochet were definitely not bite-sized portions. So what if the chef's batterie undoubtedly includes a tin opener for entrées and desserts – the main courses are all solidly home-made. Be prepared to share your table – no one stands on ceremony. A jug of water is constantly refilled, and the wine list runs from 28-55f per bottle!

A la Frégate
(R)SM   *35 q. Voltaire, 42 61 23 77, V (rue du Bac)*

There is not much choice of quayside dining along this stretch of the Seine, by the Musée d'Orsay. So the basic brasserie restaurant tradition of this old style corner restaurant has a market for its grand-mère specialities – basic grillades and poulet rôti is the staple fare. And daily specialities, such as a passable bouillabaisse marseillaise reflect the nautical name and the traditional decor. Pay under 100f for a snack meal, around 200f for restaurant dinner.

Le Jardin
(R)S   *100 r. du Bac, 42 22 81 56, V, open until 9.30 pm, cl Sun (rue du Bac)*

If France has one obsession to match its love of restaurants, it must be the joy of pharmacies. Try to imagine any other country where a crossroads has a chemist at each corner. At the pharmacy the national hypochondria is pampered and respected; one can pay for attention and old-style service; one can take one's freshly picked mushrooms for analysis, and one's poodle for a tonic. So it had to happen. A homeopathic health shop, packed with elixirs and cures, with its own restaurant at the back. Two national passions in one. The restaurant has fashionably rough plastered and whitewashed walls rather in the style of a religious retreat, but is prettily finished; the simple and light menu contains a range of set meals at 52, 70 and 96f, graded for fat and calorie counts, and shaped to specific dietary requirements. The hot dish of the day is very much selon le marché, but standard summer favourites include a refreshing terrine de fromage frais aux légumes. An ideal lunch venue the day of, or after, a gastronomic blow-out supper.

➤ L'Arpège
(R)ML   *84 r. de Varenne, 45 51 47 33, cl Sat and Sun lunch (Invalides/Varenne)*

Don't be put off by the austere façade, nor by the unexciting decor inside. You're here for the food and Paris' newest star chef, Alain Passard, is unlikely to disappoint. Passard's secret (one of the hardest to achieve) is quality ingredients served at their simplest. I tested him to the full with an unexciting sounding slice of tuna served in a spiced butter sauce – so simple, so sublime. Companion opted for the unusual combination of lobster and turnip – pronounced exquisite.

Clearly not the place for a serious conversation: the food demands
your full attention. Dessert was an indulgent mille feuilles au whisky.
Service is young, relaxed and unfussy – perhaps not to everyone's
liking in this kind of establishment, but I found the absence of starchy
waiters a relaxing bonus. Prices aren't cheap, but genius like this is a
rarity nowadays. If the lunch menu at around 170f doesn't appeal,
bank on 500f. An arrow for the outstanding quality of food at this
exciting newcomer.

Au Pied de Fouet
(R)S   *45 r. de Babylone, 47 05 12 27, cl Sat pm, Sun (Varennes or St François Xavier)*

It's rare to see spare tables at this scruffy bistro: firstly because there
are only four; secondly because this is the favourite eatery for the
locals. André, the owner, keeps personal serviettes for his many
regulars who return daily for good honest French bistro grub – soups,
casseroles, grills, at good honest prices (allow 100f all in).

La Flamberge
(R)M   *12 av. Rapp, 47 05 91 37, all cc, cl Sat, Sun (Pont l'Alma)*

This famous fish restaurant began a new régime at the end of 1992,
with the arrival of Roger Lamazère. Still with its legendary oysters and
sea-bass, I hear from my Parisian friends that the meat can now rival
the long time classics. Reports welcomed. Menu at 230f, à la carte
around 350f.

Restaurant du Musée d'Orsay
(R)S   *1 r. de Belle Chasse or 62 r. de Lille when museum is closed, 45 44 41 85,
11.30 am-2 pm and 7-9 pm on 1st floor of the museum (Solférino)*

Despite its massive proportions, the original Gare d'Orsay was up and
running within two years at the turn of the century. More palace than
railway station, with a metallic structure heavier than the Eiffel
Tower's, a 'nave' larger than Notre Dame's, the station closed 30 years
later. Not until 1975 did the French government get round to restoring,
redecorating and renovating this vast pile into the magnificent Musée
d'Orsay. You'll need a good day to do justice to the many treasures
(all enhanced by natural light). Admiring the arts needn't stop at
lunchtime. The restaurant here is a far cry from the standard dark and
dingy basement museum canteen. Elaborate Belle Epoque dominates:
gold, gilts, mirrors, marble cherubs, chandeliers throughout. The
privilege of dining here doesn't even break the bank. Pay well under
100f for a 'much as you can eat' buffet of interesting salads and
terrines, a pitcher of wine and dessert.

8th ARRONDISSEMENT

(Paris 75008)

It may just about reach Clichy in the north, and the Gare St Lazare in the east but who cares. The 8th arrondissement is French for the Champs Elysées. The quarter is as wide as the famous avenue is long, from the Arc de Triomphe to the place de la Concorde.

Prices in the quarter reflect the importance of the avenue des Champs Elysées. This is the centre of haute couture, deluxe hotels and expensive entertainment.

The avenue is undergoing a much-needed facelift at the moment; the years of fast food and fast cars have scarred the image of a

Hôtel George V

thoroughfare once considered to be the most chic in Europe. The northern section of the street, with its cinemas and arcades, is being re-landscaped, according to Le Nôtre's original design – twin rows of trees on each vast pavement, and the off-street parking consigned to new underground car parks. Even the polyurethane burger joints have been given notice to tone down their act.

The street is always packed, even at 2 am, with sightseers and high-spirited Parisians tooting their horns.

The landmarks remain. Fouquets (you pronounce the T) and the Lido have their worldwide reputations to keep them going. Below the avenue Montaigne the gardens still line the avenue shading the Grand and Petit Palais, and the Palais de l'Elysée, residence of the president.

The palace gives onto the rue du Faubourg St Honoré, an address found on the letterhead of the top boutiques and the most distinguished embassies.

The place de la Madeleine has its classical church at the centre but is truly a temple to the goddess Gluttony: Fauchon on one side of the square, with its queues of the fashionably-dressed passing through the glass doors of the chicest grocers in France; Lucas Carton on the further corner. Mid-morning sees the young commis de cuisine and kitchen porters sneaking a cigarette break on the pavement's double-sided bench; in the middle of the square, the market offers tantalising aromas to the line of theatre-goers at the half price ticket kiosk; there are wine bars, specialist food shops and the other grocery store, Hediard.

If fashionable Paris is just a little too much, there's always the river – and the Bateaux Mouches from the Pont de l'Alma.

Markets: Aguesseau, pl. de la Madeleine, Tues, Fri (Madeleine) 7 am-1.30 pm; Madeleine Flower Market, pl. de la Madeleine, Tue-Sun (Madeleine) 8 am-7.30 pm; Covered Marché Europe, r. Corveto (Villiers) Tue-Sat, 8 am-1 pm, 4-7.30 pm, Sun 8 am-1 pm; Stamp market Champs Elysées, junction with av. Marigny and av. Gabriel, Thu, Sat, Sun, Bank Holidays (Champs Elysées-Clémenceau).

HOTELS

→George V
(HR)L   *29 av. George V, 47 23 54 00, all cc (George V)*

Impossible to compile a list of Paris hotels without mentioning the most famous hotel in France. The Entrée does not usually trot out the obvious big names, but a special mention should be made of the George V, which has improved out of all recognition in the past year or so. Under the new general manager Dan Mosczytz, the once stuffy and dusty palace hotel has had a breath of fresh air. Forte's flagship is something of an art deco landmark in Paris – and over the years has hosted the great and the notorious, from Garbo, Keaton and Getty to Nixon, Peron and Maxwell. Today staff are cheerful and efficient, rooms appear brighter than before, and there is a relaxed atmosphere that permeates all corners of the hotel. The famous tapestries and wall-hangings are still very much the trademark – however, the original Picasso now resides in the safe. A harp plays at tea time and the hotel has become the headquarters of the prestigious Tea Drinkers' Club of Paris. Marriage Frères (see 4th arrondissement) have prepared a new tea-time menu for the Galérie de la Paix. In a hotel named after a British king tea is part of the fascination with things British. The tea-room also hosts a Ruth Rendell murder writing competition. Bedrooms are sumptuous and luxurious. Spacious bathrooms with snuggly robes and large towels as well as the usual toiletries and hair-dryer. Suites are very comfortable, some even have private terraces. Off-season deals with tour operators (such as Travelscene) come up with flight and accommodation packages that work out well below the official rates. Guests in suites, or on special packages, may find George V Cologne in the bathrooms and extra flowers and champagne in the bedrooms. The official room rate is from 2,850f per night. Breakfast at 115f is very disappointing – extras cost a fortune. You can have a pretty good dinner elsewhere for the price. So only take breakfast if it is included in a special offer deal. There are now two restaurants: the new grill has a reasonably priced menu at 198f, with an eye on the health conscious business luncher. Seafood is a speciality and wine may be served by the glass. A pianist plays in the evenings and the mirrored restaurant is open until 1 am. The main salon, Les Princes, had a facelift in summer 1992 and now serves lunch and dinner in a setting of cheery frescoes and soft draperies: brighter decor, and lighter cuisine. Under the guidance of executive chef, Pierre Larapide, the restaurant is beginning to win favourable whispers. Good fish dishes, an honourable mention for the lotte rôtie au cidre, served with sliced apple and spinach, and fair desserts, a modest crème grillée aux fraises, appear on a 350f three-course menu, wine and coffee included. A 450f menu dégustation includes the speciality soufflé au citron vert en chaud-froid de fruits rouges. I dined there in late August and the meal, if not yet memorable, augered well for the future. The arrow goes to the hotel for picking itself up, and making a real effort to provide value for the de luxe budget.

➤ Les Suites St Honoré

(H)L   *13 r. d'Aguesseau, 44 51 16 35, all cc (Madeleine)*

Luxury hotels never really let you live a charmed life – but a sumptuous private apartment in the heart of the richest quarter is something quite different. Almost opposite the British Embassy and just around the corner from the Elysée Palace is an excellently refurbished building housing just 13 superb private apartments. The Suites St Honoré, under the direction of the wonderful Betty Bougaud, are all different sizes and different styles. The top level duplexes, with their roof terraces, are ultra modern, but I prefer the classic apartments on the lower floors. Decorated to an excellent standard, even the smallest suite is bigger than the average Parisian home. A comfortable bedroom with picture frames at the bedside (a homely touch), a marbled bathroom with porcelain bowls of cotton buds and cotton wool as well as the usual soaps and shampoos. A second luxury shower room, and another cloakroom by the front door. In place of a second bedroom I opted for an office with fax, telephone, stylish furniture – including a sofa bed. The main living room is huge, expensively and expansively furnished with TV, video, hi-fi, even a CD player. The dining table may be set with fine place settings, for a meal prepared in the fully fitted kitchen. A huge fridge-freezer, cooker, coffee-maker and microwave, as well as all the utensils. There is a dishwasher as well – you don't even have to switch it on; the discreet staff pop in to clean up whenever you nip out to the shops. Shopping is wonderful as the Suites are midway between the Faubourg St Honoré (posh frocks) and the place de la Madeleine (posh snacks)

Suites St Honoré

from Fauchon – see below – and the good street market for fresh foods. What I love about the suites is that I can actually take advantage of the good food shopping and create a dinner party for two or twenty in the comfort of my own home. Suites can double as conference meeting rooms, whilst allowing the family freedom to enjoy half the apartment without butting in on business. There is no restaurant on site, but Betty's super-efficient staff can bring in outside caterers to your apartment in the blinking of an eye. The 90f continental breakfast is great value with neither jam nor butter served pre-packed. Rates, irrespective of the number of occupants, from just 2,000f per night for my apartment, to 4,200f for two double bedrooms and an office-bedroom. Rates are substantially lower for stays of more than 6 nights. If you are budgeting for a Palace Hotel stay, then the suites offer an irresistible challenge to the anonymity of an hotel. Arrowed for quality and service.

→Hôtel de l'Elysée
(H)M   *12 r. des Saussaies, 42 65 29 25 (Miromesnil or Champs Elysées)*

Guests from the Hotel Ferrandi (see 6th arrondissement) will recognise the decor and welcoming smiles at the Hôtel de l'Elysée. The industrious Madame Lafond runs both establishments with a professional and caring eye. The Elysée is the more opulent of the two – Italianate frescoes adorn the magnificent 19th-century stairway. Downstairs is more British – wood panelling and welcoming log fires. Rooms are spacious (specially those with numbers ending in 1 or 4), some flowery, others more sober, with furniture dating from mid-19th century. Matching bedspreads, headboards and curtains tend to overwhelm in some rooms. Prices are good, bearing in mind the location (just a stone's throw from the Champs Elysées), ranging from 500-900f for a double. If money allows, ask for one of the two suites which have been restored at the top of the building (1,250f, advanced booking usually necessary). An arrow goes to the Elysée for its location, service and good value in an area where many hotels have indulged in sky-high prices.

Madeleine Plaza
(H)M   *33 pl. de la Madeleine, 42 65 20 63, SE MC V (Madeleine)*

Reasonably priced (470f) rooms on the place de la Madeleine itself, are something of a bargain. Clean bedrooms with bland inoffensive decor overlook the church and the food market.

RESTAURANTS

Boissier
(ST)L   *46 av. Marceau*

Very old, very chic, very established, very snob address for your afternoon cuppa. But you pay for it – from 70f upwards.

Le Fermette Marboeuf 1900

(R)M   *5 r. Marboeuf, 47 20 63 53, all cc, open all year (Alma Marceau)*

Visitors to no. 5 rue Marboeuf pre-1978 will recall little more than a
self-service snack bar serving plastic food in plastic surroundings. 15
years ago the builders discovered behind the formica walls a treasure
trove of art nouveau ceramics, columns and stained glass. In 1982
M. Laurent, now the proud owner of this mini-museum piece,
painstakingly transferred 5,000 stained glass panes one by one from a
country home in the Parisian suburbs into what is now the exquisite
back room. M. Laurent could easily over-charge his visitors for the
privilege of spending a few hours in such exceptional surroundings,
all just a diamond's throw from the Hôtel George V. Fortunately for
the budgeting tourist his prices are still good value with an excellent
menu under 200f. Food is innovative and occasionally 'nouvelle'.
Calf's tongue cooked in Sauterne and served with a delicate aubergine
mousse was original and delicious; friend's plateau de fruits de mer
was piled high and excellent value. Wines are varied with a good
selection of Bordeaux at reasonable prices. Allow about 300f à la
carte.

Fouquet's

(R)ML   *99 av. des Champs Elysées, 47 23 70 60, all cc (George V)*

Now saved and listed as a national monument, it is a pity something
could not have been done to restore the kitchen to its former glory.
Sadly, the food appears to have lost its culinary edge – the new
branch at the Bastille has the verve and fire that once characterised
this oh-so-chic restaurant. Decor is still great, and the steaks and fish
dishes are OK – but not what they were. Women are not allowed to
stand alone at the bar (unbelievable) but even from a seat on the
terrace – the best option for those who just wish to say they've *been*
here – you can see the politicos and ageing rockers whose very
presence still turns heads. Whatever happens to the Champs Elysées,
Fouquet's will always remain the premier address for people-
watching.

Le Bistrot du Sommelier

(R)M   *9 bd. Haussmann (Chaussée d'Antin)*

As the name suggests, this is one of the best places in town to really
understand and learn about that important relationship between food
and wine. Owner, Philippe Faure, is a worldwide respected sommelier.
One of his latest and much approved innovations is his 350f 'menu
dégustation' which offers you the chance to sample six dishes
specially prepared to complement six different wines.

La Coupole du Printemps
(R)S   *6th floor, Printemps, bd. Haussmann, MC V AE (Auber)*

Rarely does a Parisian visit go by without an indulgent morning in the 'Grands Magazins' department stores of boulevard Haussmann – the Selfridges, bordering on Harrods of Paris. Just when the legs begin to tire, Printemps has a treat in store up on the 6th floor at La Coupole. This is not your average department store self-service canteen with formica tables. The Coupole (for snacks) and Brasserie Flo (starchy brasserie) are worth a recce whatever the state of your appetite. Striking art nouveau decor makes a simple lunch a pleasure. For a snack with a view, climb a further two floors to the 8th floor café with a panorama over Parisian rooftops – outside terrace dining in summer.

Fauchon
(ST)   *30 pl. de la Madeleine (Madeleine)*

One look at the number of noses pressed up against the window is a clue to the teatime masterpieces on display inside. This is *the* place to get your going-home presents: beautifully packaged teas and coffees

Fauchon

downstairs, and calorific creations in the salon de thé. Fauchon's worldwide reputation has placed it on many a tourist itinerary, so be prepared to wait with fellow foreigners.

La Maison du Chocolat
(ST)   *52 r. François 1er (Franklin D Roosevelt)*

The chocoholics' paradise. Owner Robert Linxe knows every calorific detail there is to know about this much-loved vice. Take it in liquid form, hot and frothy, or in the guise of truffles, gâteaux or biscuits. Waitresses advise on the many different vintages and varieties available.

Chez André
(R)M   *12 r. Marboeuf, 47 20 59 57, MC V (Franklin D Roosevelt)*

The staff are charming and fun, a legacy of the old days, but today Monsieur Pierre, son of the founding André, is here no longer. Nonetheless, the food is as good as ever, with nostalgic favourites such as the gigot and tête de veau still going. I've a friend who goes regularly for the delicious oeuf en gelée. The wine list does justice to the standard fare. Brouilly in a 50cl carafe at around 70f brings the cost of a meal to about 230f.

L'Ecluse
(R)S   *15 pl. de la Madeleine, 42 65 34 69 (Madeleine)*

In the gastronomic wonderland that is the place Madeleine, you might be forgiven for overlooking l'Ecluse surrounded as it is by the great temples of food from Fauchon (the Fortnum and Mason's of Paris – see above) and the 800f a head bill of fare at Lucas Carton, to the street markets of cheeses and vegetables around the church. You might be forgiven, but would you forgive yourself. I doubt it. This wine bar specialises in the tastes of Bordeaux, and serves the good crus by the glass: Château Muranc Maillet Pomerol 1985 at 32f. To enjoy the wine, taste another Bordelais speciality. Spend 75f on a steak tartare or less on my favourite – chavignol and cucumber in olive oil and herbs. All this is of course merely an excuse to pig out on the gâteau de chocolat 'comme au début' as it is listed on the menu to reassure old customers returning to the bar. There are Parisians who swear that this is the best choccy mouthful in the city – who am I to disagree?

→ L'Entrecôte
(R)S   *29 r. Marignan, 42 25 28 60, all cc, open until 1 am (Franklin D Roosevelt)*

No reservations taken, so it's best to get here early for this Parisian legend just off the Champs Elysées. Legendary for the extent of the menu: a choice of one. Your first course is a light green salad, and the main course the eponymous entrecôte, prepared at the table in its delicious Café de Paris sauce, the exact recipe of which is the restaurant's closely guarded secret. Part of the fun of the meal is analysing the aromatic sauce, and guessing its constituents. It is served with pommes alumettes 'à volonté'. The two courses come to 78f, desserts are around the 30f mark and basic wine under 90f a bottle. Arrowed for reliability and value.

Café de Paris

(R)SM   70-76 av. des Champs Elysées, MC V, open every day to 8 pm, Sat 1 am, Sun 10 pm, no telephone for reservations (Franklin D Roosevelt)

Appearances can be deceptive. I've dismissed the arcades as mere tourist traps. Now I know better. This glass-topped shopping arcade has the restaurant where the mere mortals who work in shops and offices along the pricey Champs go for a nourishing and reliable lunch. Seats fill the central aisle of the arcade. Go for the simple brasserie fare. The filets de hareng aux pommes tièdes is always excellent value at 28f, and such specials as the pot au feu du poisson are mouthwateringly moreish. Portions are always generous – the waitress joked about selling me a rabbit to help me finish an enormous salad. Budget on paying 150f for lunch with house wine or beer.

Pizza Pino

(R)S   31 av. des Champs Elysées, 43 59 23 89, all cc, open until 5 am (Franklin D Roosevelt)

A cautionary mention of this branch of the usually reliable Paris Italian chain. Those who have eaten in the good value Les Halles branch might fancy a bite here. The identical menu is priced higher for the richer tourist clientele of the Champs. Not only that, but on a recent visit, I was handed a menu that was priced even higher than the prices displayed outside. The reason given was that as it was getting late, the night-time charges were now in operation. I have no objection to a slight increase in charges after midnight or 1 am. But the time of my visit was 2.20 in the afternoon.

➤Yvan

(R)M   1 bis r. Jean-Mermoz, 43 59 18 40, all cc, cl Sat lunch, Sun (Franklin D Roosevelt)

You cannot compete with Yvan's for value for money – lunch menu just 178f, on the Champs Elysées. And the other four set deals range from 168-278f. Given the location, Yvan Zaplatilek could charge far more, but instead he concentrates on providing good food. Creditable St Jacques, excellent rognons de veau, usually given an imaginative twist from the herb garden and spice jar. The decor is somewhat ad-agency modern, but the waiters slip from table to table with a classic ease and professionalism. Arrowed for value.

Marshalls
(R)M   *63 av. Franklin D Roosevelt, 45 63 21 22, all cc (St Philippe du Roule)*

Madame Ganem knows her Parisians. The French adore America, so the upmarket 8th arrondissement needs an upmarket burger bar. Though, to be fair, Marshalls is no McDonalds. It is a Californian restaurant that takes popular modern North American standards and gives them a Parisian flair. Thus the back section of the restaurant has the branché business lunchers enjoying their foie gras burgers and healthy, delicious salads. It takes a Frenchwoman to provide the best showcase for American cuisine in a district that is battling to rid itself of the fast-food transatlantic invasion. No set menu, but pay around 250f.

Aux Amis du Beaujolais
(R)S   *28 r. d'Artois, 45 63 92 21, V MC [over 100f] (St Philippe du Roule)*

Hearty fare in a bright modern corner restaurant. Local shop and office workers in this Faubourg St Honoré quarter opt for the realistic prices and open-minded approach to traditional food – from andouillettes to paupiettes de veau – rather than the more pretentious establishments nearby. The menu changes daily; expect to pay around 100-120f for food, between 80-140f for a Beaujolais cru.

Le Restaurant
(R)M   *41 r. du Colisée, 45 63 15 02, cl Sat lunch, Sun (St Philippe du Roule)*

At around 230f à la carte, one can mingle with the darling set of television and theatre personalities who dine acceptably well after the theatre. Late last orders, at around 1.30 am, make it an honest option after the floor show at the Lido. Go for the ratatouille niçoise and the veal kidneys.

Bateaux Mouches
(R)L   *Pont de l'Alma, 42 25 96 10, all cc (Alma Marceau)*

For years I dismissed the bateaux mouches as mere tourist traps on water – then I was taken out for my birthday. As well as being the best river tour of the city, with illustrated route maps on the table, and excellent floodlighting, they provide a pretty acceptable meal. Lunch is 300f for the 1 hour 45 minute tour (350f on Sundays). Dinner is 500f and there is the option of dinner-dance as well. Children pay half price. Four- or five-course meals include a savoury and moreish coulibiac of salmon and roast quail. Portions are generous, vegetarians well catered for, house wine incuded with the meal, and a modest additional wine selection that ranges from a '66 Margaux at 750f to a 300f Chablis 1er cru. Accordionists play during the meal – requests are welcomed.

9th ARRONDISSEMENT

(Paris 75009)

Oh, les grands boulevards! The story is the same as for the 2nd arrondissement. And though the boulevards des Capucines and Italiens may seem identical on both sides of the road, the streets to the north in the 9th arrondissement are very different to those spreading southward through the 2nd.

This quarter from the Madeleine and Opéra to the Faubourg Poissonnière, owes more to its neighbours in the north – the boulevard de Clichy – than to its fashionable partners in the south. It is a district dedicated to pleasure, from the harmless joys of shopping along the boulevard Haussmann, with Galeries Lafayette and Printemps spread through multiple buildings and pavement traders, through the theatres on the boulevards and around the church of Trinité, to the razzle-dazzle nightlife.

The sleaze of Clichy – a district shared with the 18th arrondissement – offers a thousand neon promises. Nearer the grands boulevards are the floorshows of the Folies Bergères, and nightclubs, such as the Palace on the Faubourg Montmartre, where supermodels and millionaires get in free. Poor visitors are lucky to be allowed in, paying hundreds of francs for the privilege!

Near rue Montmartre metro station is the city's only all night news kiosk – a point to remember for solitary diners who, like me, cannot endure a lone late-night snack without a magazine propped on the cruet.

Shopping is more practical here than in the pricy St Honoré and Champs Elysées districts. Those two main department stores have the tourist market pretty well sewn up, leaving free city maps and 10% discount vouchers in most hotels.

During longer stays, the stores' free fashion shows are worth a visit. One of my favourite memories of Paris is of the traditional finale at Galeries Lafayette. The first fairy-tale wedding dress was followed by an outrageous catwalk confection of split skirt, slashed chiffon, backless, strapless, off-the-shoulder audacity, with décolletage that could have been designed as a hemline. Behind me, a Yorkshire woman, shopping for her daughter's trousseau, drew a breath and muttered, 'I give that marriage three months!'

HOTELS

Hôtel du Leman
(H)M   *20 r. Trévise, 42 46 50 66, all cc (rue Montmartre)*

Any closer to the Folies Bergères and it would be in the front row of the chorus, the Leman nestles in that corner of the 9th that is the shared province of three-star tourist hotels and kosher delis. Other guides have waxed lyrical about the breakfast served here – deserved praise as the small but bright cellar hosts a fresh fruit buffet, choice of cheese and cereals as well as the standard coffee, croissants and baguettes. The cheery staff offer eggs, boiled, fried or scrambled as part of the good value 40f petit déjeuner. Would that the rest of the hotel was up to this standard. Rooms are charged at 450-800f, and my 540f bedroom, though modern in decor, had mismatched bed linen and was shared with a discreet colony of ants.

Hôtel Bergère
(H)M   *34 r. Bergère, 47 70 34 34, all cc (rue Montmartre)*

Decor is fine, but staff unbending and cold, in this smartly finished hotel aiming squarely at the international tourist market. Standard international three-star anonymity.

Les Hôtels de la Cité Bergère
(H)SM   *off rues Bergère and Faubourg Montmartre (rue Montmartre)*

This charming little street is a particular novelty of the quarter. Narrow archways take the visitor into a little private L-shaped lane lined with two- and three-star hotels. All have grand frontages and are nicely

L'Hôtel des Arts

dated – as opposed to repro 'period' – in style: carpets often just a little too thin, light bulbs with that low wattage exclusive to French hotels. All in all, exactly what one remembers from early first visits to Paris. The fact that the road is effectively closed to through traffic means that the nights are far quieter than one would expect in this noisy night-clubbing district. My personal choice would be: **Hôtel des Arts** at number 7 (tel: 42 46 73 30). A simple two-star hotel with a cheery welcome, chirpy parrot and lots of flowers and plants outside. The rooms, sensibly priced at around the 350f mark for doubles. Three-star alternatives, but rather more tourist class, despite room rates over 500f, are the **Hôtel Victoria** at number 2 bis (tel: 47 70 20 01) and the **Hôtel Mondial**, at number 5 (tel: 47 70 55 56). All take Mastercard, Visa and Amex.

Florence
(H)M   *26 r. des Mathurins, 47 42 63 47, all cc (Havre Caumartin)*

Madame Fabre runs this Florence, but it is her spaniel that provides the first welcome as he rushes to greet newcomers to this 20-room hotel, conveniently situated by the twin food hall temples of the Opéra district – Galleries Lafayettes for the British, and Marks and Spencer for the French. They may just serve breakfast these days, but once upon a time there was always a chicken in the pot. Before Haussmann altered the shape of the streets, this was the home of Napoleon's cook who, according to Mme Fabre, was obliged permanently to have a chicken prepared to rush round to the imperial table day or night. In 1822-26 Georges Sand lived here. Not that you could tell from the style of the rooms: bland, simple, clean and (those facing the road) double-glazed. I sat up all night watching the British election on cable TV, and the morning clarion of traffic did not penetrate my eventual doze. Rooms are 550f.

Havane
(H)M   *44 r. de Trévise, 47 70 79 12, all cc (Cadet)*

Between the department stores and the main line stations, this popular little hotel has been a choice of independent travel agents for some time. Their guests are in good hands. Helpful staff, good standard rooms – with private safes – and prices from around 400f.

Pavia
(H)S   *29 r. de la Bruyère, 48 74 50 60, AE MC V (St Georges)*

Budget hotel with rooms from under 300f; all is clean and tidy and some of the bedrooms are surprisingly spacious. Situated midway between the Boulevards and Pigalle, the hotel is convenient for theatres and nightlife. The rooms are even better value when the hotel takes part in the Bon Weekend promotion (see page •••).

RESTAURANTS

→**Chartier**
(R)S   7 r. de Faubourg Montmartre, 47 70 86 29, no cc, open 11 am-3 pm,
6.30-9 pm (rue Montmartre)

The arrow is neither for the food nor the service, but for being so
Parisian. Here you find the decor, menu and arrogance that makes a
genuine institution. You can't book, you can't sit where you want and
you can't spend ages mulling over the menu. But still you'll join the
queue down the passageway to the little courtyard that is Chartier – a
students' soup kitchen off a brasserie that offers almost unrivalled
value for money. Little has changed since it first appeared in the *Guide
Bleu* 100 years ago. Still the stuccos, the gilts, the brass coat rack and

Le Bistrot du Curé

the polished wood. And the food is as reliable as ever: pot au feu, crispy roast chicken served with crisp pommes frites. Your brisk and harassed waiter will hover no longer than it takes to scrawl your choice on the paper tablecloth. And the prices are so low (8f for potage du jour, 35f a main course, rarely more than 75f for a substantial three courses) that who cares if you are forced to share with three total strangers.

Le Bistrot du Curé
(R)S   *21 bd. de Clichy, 48 74 65 84, cl Sun and religious holidays (Pigalle)*

Only Paris could nurture a Bistro du Curé. Once upon a time there was a disgraceful quarter called Pigalle. Here ladies of the night walked the streets – even during the day. Nestling in the heart of Paris' naughty nightlife, sandwiched between the Sexodrome peep show and a leather and latex emporium, is the unlikely success story of the quarter. Founded by local churchmen, who realised that a parish in the neon twilight of Montmartre and Pigalle is hardly likely to boast the most conventional of parishioners, the bistro was established as a missionary outpost in the Clichy underworld. Providing a nourishing meal at very low prices, the bistro attracts surely Paris' most mixed clientele. Prostitutes, transvestites and the colourful characters of the sex clubs and strip shows mix with showgirls, students and passing tourists. The waiting staff usually includes at least one priest, but there is no tableside proselytising. The church wanted only to show the local community that it accepts all its members. However, the duty cleric is available for quiet consultation away from the dining room. Value and traditional good food is the key to the restaurant's success. A plat du jour and dessert will cost just 38f. There are menus at 53f and 85f, and the bill of fare usually follows the faux filet, coq au vin, pot au feu standard. The bar serves no alcohol.

➤Le Petit Batailley
(R)M   *26 r. Bergère, 47 70 85 81, all cc, cl Sat lunch and Sun, Aug (rue Montmartre)*

Bernard Martin and his chef, Serge Hacquet, reprint their nice clean menus every fortnight, an attention to the market and detail typical of this tiny corner of provincial France in the cosmopolitan quarter of Thai, Lebanese and Kosher alternatives. This is a restaurant where the decor is all brown walls and pink linen, and the food of the quality that does not strike the clientele dumb with awe, but ignites a gentle hum of contentment throughout the room. M. Martin catches the elusive balance between business lunch and romantic dinner. Food is traditional with an original edge. The amuse-gueule of salmon and mustard, the beef and coriander terrine, and the moist and tender duo de poisson in a delicious beurre blanc. The three-course menu is 139f, including flavoursome desserts à la carte. A gastronomique menu is just 205f, and that features the house's much appreciated foie gras. A la carte would be around 250f. A simple wine list, with inexpensive suggestions – I was offered a chilled red Graves to accompany a rich fish meal. The arrow is for not being Parisian.

→La Table d'Anvers
(R)ML   *2 pl. d'Anvers, 48 78 35 21, AE MC V, cl Sat lunch, Sun, Aug (Anvers)*

Don't plan to break important news over dinner here – you'll never get around to it. The food takes over. The cooking even upstages the Sacré Coeur up the road. The boned pigeon sounded simple, but when it melted into the Banyuls sauce, my companions simpered, and I was won over by a lip-smacking turbot with bayleaves. All these and more, such as the ruffian au homard and selle d'agneau rôtie au romarin et abricots secs, both of which we were recommended, alas as yet untried (reports welcome), created by Christian Conticini. His brother, Philippe, has been described as among Paris' finest pastry chefs, and the evidence of the dessert menu only reinforces the reputation. Take the Dacquoise, his confection of meringue and almonds, and countless variations on puff pastry, chocolate and creams. Pricewise, lunch can be a mere 190f, if you stick to the menu, and set meals range from 280-490f. Wine, alas, is not as good value, so budget around 250f a bottle. Arrowed for good food.

La Poste
(R)L   *34 r. Duperré, 42 80 66 16, V MC, open until 1 am, cl Sun/Aug (Pigalle)*

Lavish renovation of this 19th century house wherein, it is said, Bizet wrote Carmen, gives a clue to the prices. Budget 500-600f a head for dinner in the Pigalle quarter. The food (light and luxe) is very good, but at these prices I suspect one is paying for the fashionable clientele who flock to the patron, designer Michel Axel.

L'Olympic
(R)SM   *11 r. du Faubourg Montmartre, 47 70 85 69, open until 3.30 am (rue Montmartre)*

Cuisine familiale, but what a family of customers. An improbable mix of the beautiful people and the pennywise keep this noisy and bustling little eatery packed in the small hours. Its location opposite the fashionable discotheque Le Palace means that hungry supermodels rub elbows with us lesser mortals, for a late night refuelling of pavé au roquefort or coq au vin. The current menu is painted on the mirrored walls lining the narrow dining room. Pay around 100f.

Le Diable au Thym
(R)SM   *35 r. Bergère, 47 70 77 09, cl Sat lunch and Sun evenings in winter (rue Montmartre)*

Small modern restaurant offering acceptably populist fare on the tagliatelle de saumon, tarte au mirabelle style. Pay around 100-150f.

Au Petit Riche
(R)M   *25 r. le Peletier, 47 70 68 68, all cc, cl Sun and holidays (Richelieu Drouot)*

A century back, this was the domain of the Parisian petits riches (bourgeois) who would take their promenade down the nearby Grands Boulevards, flaunting their wealth for all to see before retiring to some elegant dining room. Not a lot has changed since – service, decor and food are neat, safe and polished, starched serviettes and tablecloths are whiter than white, silver and glasses cleaned to glistening, red velvet upholstery reminiscent of century-old rail carriages. Less than 200f for the menu brings a three-course menu including wine (lunch only) was good value for a restaurant of this quality. The warm kidney salad, duck breast cooked in Chinon wine and succulent tarte aux pommes were faultless in presentation, quantity and taste. Most dishes have a Touraine influence, as do the wines: 76f for a very drinkable Muscadet or 57f for a carafe of house wine. Many theatre-goers (a large proportion of the clientele) opt for the good value theatre package – 300f for theatre tickets and an à la carte dinner. My one gripe is the welcome – unnecessarily dour and solemn, with service at times embarrassingly pretentious. But few seem to care judging by its popularity – booking advisable.

Le Bistrot des Deux Théâtres
(R)M   *18 r. Blanche, 45 26 41 43, MC V, open daily until 12.30 am (Trinité)*

As its name implies, ideal for late-night/post-theatre eating in the Montmartre/Pigalle area. The Casino de Paris and the Théâtre Mogador are just along the road – both houses famed for Parisian or Broadway versions of international musicals. It has served me well post *Cats, Les Misérables* and *Peter Pan* over the years: reliable, efficient, good value – no surprises from the kitchen, just classic French cooking. My fresh salmon served with 'beurre nantais' sauce was cooked to perfection. The three-course 160f menu includes apéritif and a very drinkable Côtes du Rhône.

Au Pupillon
(R)S   *19 r. Notre Dame de Lorette, 42 85 46 06, MC V, cl Sat and Sun lunch (St Georges or Notre Dame de Lorette)*

One of those French perks that we Brits tend to covet – cheap and unpretentious eateries with interesting grub – ideal if you don't want to act the ripped-off tourist in the Montmartre area up the road. Service and welcome are relaxed, verging occasionally on the cool and laid back. Clientele are young and similarly cool and laid back. Upstairs infinitely prettier than down – all is salmon pink dotted with posters and contemporary paintings. Just two menus to choose from: the three course for less than 150f or two dishes for well under 100f,

Maison de la Franche Comte

both excellent value, both with lots of choice. I dined on a spinach salad accompanied with creamy fourme d'ambert cheese, my companion on chicken livers served in a subtle chive sauce, polished off with a creamy dark chocolate mousse. Reasonably-priced wines accompany – 70f for a delicious Gamay.

Le Franche Comte
(R)SM   2 bd. de la Madeleine, 49 24 99 09, AE MC V, cl Sun (Madeleine)

If only all tourist offices were as good as this. Behind the regional brochure counters plugging France's least known (to the British) region, is a restaurant serving the specialities of the various streams, farms and vineyards of the area. A range of menus from 82-175f as well as a varied carte, includes a low calorie special at 110f. I went for the regional dégustation menu, starting with a fricassée of wild mushrooms, followed by a disappointing poached trout au savagnin; the soufflé glacé au kirsch was good enough, but the highlight of the meal was the comte AOC, a king of hard cheeses. Pasteur may be the region's most famous son, but the cheeses are suitably unpasteurised. A really helpful waiter talked me through the wine list, and his recommendation, a 1988 Côtes du Jura at 120f, was delicious. Reservations essential during the week, as the bankers of the Opéra district like to keep the place to themselves!

➤ Charlot Roi des Coquillages
(R)M   81 bd. de Clichy, 48 74 49 64, all cc, open till 1 am (place de Clichy)

Not to be confused with Charlot 1er (18th arrondissement) across the road. Something of an institution, this seafood brasserie. Rich visitors opt for one of the many lobster dishes, locals go for a platter of seafood and natter over the shells late at night. The real reason for a trip to Charlot is the legendary bouillabaisse, that somehow brings the sleazy Clichy district that much closer to Marseille. Since the place had a good clean up in the late eighties, a fashionable after-theatre crowd joins the post-Moulin Rouge parties. The lunch menu is 250f including wine. Evenings, expect to shell out around 400f for the full works.

Tea Follies
(ST)S   6 pl. Gustave Toudouze, 42 80 08 44 (Pigalle)

A good snack shop in this touristy area. Throughout the day, Tea Follies serves its many regulars – a mixture of students (prices are low), artists, intellectuals and business women (good for diet lunches) – a range of teas, salads and sandwiches. Good for Sunday brunch.

10th ARRONDISSEMENT

(Paris 75010)

From the grands boulevards and République to the boulevard de la Chapelle is the territory of the quarter that introduces most visitors to Paris.

The Gares de Nord and de l'Est are at the centre of the 10th. The former is the terminus for trains from London. Even those travelling by air will take the RER rail link from the airport to the Gare du Nord.

The stations are surrounded by pizza parlours, sandwich bars and burger emporia, but cross a few main roads and this noisy but cheerful quarter will show its own character soon enough. The Canal St Martin can be picked up here, before it winds through the 19th arrondissement.

Markets: r. Alibert, Tue, Fri (Goncourt) 7 am-1.30 pm; covered Marché St Martin, 31-33 r. Château d'Eau (Château d'Eau) and Marché St Quentin, 85 bis bd. Magenta (Gare de l'Est) both Tue-Sat 8 am-1 pm, 4-7.30 pm, Sun 8 am-1 pm.

HOTELS

Français
(H)M   *13 r. du 8 mai 1945, 40 35 94 14, V MC AE (Gare de l'Est)*

This large station hotel almost opposite the Gare de l'Est, and just round the corner from the Gare du Nord, is surprisingly friendly and welcoming – a smile at the reception, a reasonable room rate and modernised rooms well fitted and equipped. International satellite TV, safes in the bedroom, piped radio in the nicely tiled bathrooms, unsurprising in the L class, is remarkable value at around 400f. As the bedrooms are gradually refurbished, the hotel expands its programme of fleurissement; trees on each of the balconies at the front of the hotel, and shrubs and tubs outside rear-facing rooms on the first floor. Breakfast may be taken in an attractive ground floor salon.

Terminus Nord
(H)M   *12 bd. de Denain, 42 80 20 00, all cc (Gare du Nord)*

No amount of refurbishment could disguise this warren – it remains resolutely a railway traveller's rest. Negotiating the maze of corridors to the bedroom could well qualify guests for the Duke of Edinburgh Bronze award in orienteering. Nothing quaint or nostalgic here. Rooms are stolidly old fashioned, with large baths and broad upright basins. But the location, immediately opposite the Gare du Nord, is prime, being 25 minutes from the airport, and a TGV away from the Channel ports. Unfortunately breakfast is not taken in the celebrated

Hôtel Terminus Nord

ground floor brasserie (see separate listing below), but in a bright first
floor room overlooking the busy rue Dunkerque. Rooms cost in the
region of 500f.

Suède
(H)M   *106 bd Magenta, 40 36 10 12, V MC (Gare du Nord)*

430f buys a double room at this smart modern Scandinavian-style
hotel. Efficient staff and an attractive lounge make it a cut above some
of the standard small station hotels along the boulevard Magenta.

L'Europe
(H)M   *98 bd. Magenta, 40 37 71 15, V MC (Gare du Nord)*

Basic accommodation, helpful staff and a location almost directly
opposite the indoor Marché St Quentin. Pay 330f for a double room.

Windsor Opera
(H)L   *10 r. Gabriel Laumain, 48 00 98 98, all cc (Bonne Nouvelle)*

At more than 750f a double room, the hotel is not cheap, but during off-season weekends it is a member of the Bon Weekend promotion, which offers two nights for the price of one. Off the Faubourg Poissonnière near the business district of the Grands Boulevards, it has been modernised by the new owners who have also double-glazed the windows. Hair-dryer, satellite TV and mini-bar are standard in the good-sized rooms, with big windows in the bathrooms. A friendly welcome, but go during the discount season.

Lille
(H)S   *2 r. Montholon, 47 70 38 76, no cc (Poissonnière)*

Rooms with en suite facilities at 200f are a bargain in this basic, clean hotel which recently double-glazed all front windows. No extras, but flowers in windows facing the rue Montholon on the first and second floors. Rooms on the fifth floor have tiny balconies with planted shrubs as a consolation for the long walk upstairs – there's no lift.

RESTAURANTS

Chez Michel
(R)ML   *10 r. de Belzunce, 48 78 44 14, V MC AE, cl weekends (Gare du Nord)*

Just a hop and a skip from the gastronomic minefield that surrounds the Gare du Nord, where acceptable pizza joints jostle amongst the fat food and fast buck merchants, is a tranquil oasis across the boulevard Magenta. The rue de Belzunce, behind the church of St Vincent de Paul, boasts a fair choice of dining – the gourmet laurels go to Chez Michel, where serious cuisine is served in the timbered, draped and studded dining room. Foie de veau was enriched and sharpened with the flavours of honey and lemon, and a fricassée de volaille came with a distinctive twist of tarragon. Sauces are something of a speciality – even a modest beurre blanc has a true finesse. Prices are pretty high, however, and at about 500f à la carte, bargain-hunters will be disappointed. Consolation comes in the limited lunch menu at 175f.

Chez Casimir
(R)SM   *6 r. de Belzunce, 48 78 32 53, all cc, cl weekend (Gare du Nord)*

If the cuisine is not as haute as Michel's along the road, this place is far more relaxed. I was irresistibly reminded of the dining room of a provincial logis, first by the decor – hints of la chasse and brick walls papered with hundreds of yellowing wine labels – and then by the food. This is not a chic Parisian re-interpretation of the traditional, but an unfashionably old style bistro with but four tables, around which at least five waiting staff cluck attentively. The welcome, especially to one staggering into sanctuary from the noise and confusion of the

Gare du Nord, is warm, the food simple and simply prepared in the tiny kitchen. No surprises here. Good 5A andouillettes (see Les Noces de Jeanette in the 2nd arrondissement for explanation), poisson du marché, cassoulet and moules. Vegetables are puréed into quenelles. The cheese board and dessert trolley of brightly-coloured pâtisseries – a rarity in chic Paris circles – are trundled in at the end of 300f worth of à la carte dining. The bargain is the 175f menu – four courses, including half bottle of drinkable Bordeaux – which culminates in a plate of assorted gâteaux and tartes.

Terminus Nord
(R)SM   *23 r. de Dunkerque, 42 85 05 15, all cc (Gare du Nord)*

Despite being taken over by the excellent Flo chain (see above), I am happy to report that the famous station brasserie still has the same arrogant waiters, whose superciliousness is as much a part of the tradition as the mouthwatering display of seafood outside and the brass and aspidistra decor within. Also known as the Brasserie 1925, this is a marvellous place for the final breakfast before catching the train back to London. Fresh butter croissants taste even better accompanied by tearful farewells. For years I've imagined Noel Coward and Hercule Poirot stepping off the boat train and crossing the road to sit here with friends. At mealtimes, this is a good choice for oysters and mussels and the soupière de homard à la Bretonne. Pay around 200f for a meal.

Les Deux Canards
(R)M   *8 r. du Faubourg Poissonnière, 47 70 03 32, all cc, cl Sat lunch, Sun, mid-summer (Bonne Nouvelle)*

More than two ways to serve duck here. Traditional dishes (canard à l'orange a speciality) and pleasing fish creations as well. One of the first no-smoking restaurants in Paris. Eat well for under 300f, and splash out on the good value wine list.

11th ARRONDISSEMENT

(Paris 75011)

A twilight world between the bustling city centre and the outlying dormitory quarters, the 11th arrondissement is bounded by the place de la Bastille, the place de la Nation, Belleville and the place de la République.

Although République is tucked away in a far corner of the quarter, it nonetheless gives the area its identity. Brasseries, a Holiday Inn and a branch of the wonderful Tati discount clothing store (see 19th arrondissement), surround the square itself; but further into the quarter can be found surprisingly good simple restaurants serving the local community.

The nightclubs of the Bastille infringe upon this territory, but although their postcode might be that of the 11th, they belong to the newly trendy 12th (see next section). Entertainment here can be found at the Cirque d'Hiver, a magnificent indoor circus which hosts international acts, as well as wonderful *bals publics*.

Markets: bd. de Belleville, Tue, Fri (Belleville); bd. de Charonne, Wed, Sat (Alexandre-Dumas); Père Lachaise, bd. de Ménilmontant, Tue, Fri (Père Lachaise); Popincourt, bd. Richard-Lenoir, Tue, Fri (Oberkampf); Bastille, bd. Richard Lenoir, Thu, Sun (Bastille). All 7 am-1.30 pm.

HOTELS

Home Plaza Bastille
(H)L   *74 r. Amelot, 40 21 20 00, all cc (St Sebastian)*

Billed as an all-suite hotel, the Home Plaza is actually an attractive courtyard of 18th and 19th century apartment buildings, each modernised and named after a great French figure. The 290 studios and suites are, in effect, hotel rooms with kitchenette facilities – hob and fridge – for preparing your own meals. Quite an adventure, self-catering in the city centre. The decor is modern and pleasant, but prices at upwards of 800f per night a little steep. However, should you book the hotel as part of a package with your flight or ferry crossing through a Paris brochure, or take up an off-season promotion, the room rate becomes far more reasonable. The hotel has a grill restaurant, and the Place République is but a short walk away. Beware of the name. It is at least 10 minutes from the Bastille.

Atlantide République
(H)M   *114 bd. Richard Lenoir, 43 38 29 29, all cc (Oberkampf)*

Neat and clean, with quiet sound-proofed bedrooms, the hotel has been completely renovated. Decent bathrooms and the usual three-star extras. The hotel also goes by the name of Atlantide Le Marais – but the Marais is a five-minute walk away. Double rooms with bath are 560f.

Printinia
(H)S   *16 bd. du Temple, 47 00 33 46, V MC (Filles du Calvaire)*

Just up the road from the Cirque d'Hiver and opposite the fashionable Marais is this budget hotel suitable for anyone requiring just a bed. It will not be to everyone's taste – but don't be put off by the million key scratch scrawls on the lift, or the welcoming trellis of garish plastic plants; the people who run this very basic hotel are friendly and lively. When I was half an hour late for breakfast, no one minded. The receptionist popped up the road for fresh croissants and brewed a new pot of coffee. Rooms – at around the 250f mark – are clean and contain a bed, a chair and a table. No more. Many have en suite shower cubicles. The place is creaky and the hallways in need of a paint job, but for an inexpensive place to rest a weary head, good value in the République/Marais quarter.

Notre Dame
(H)S   *51 r. du Malte, 47 00 78 76, V MC (République)*

Another basic hotel – again just the bed and a shower – still produces the welcoming touches, such as fresh flowers in the breakfast room, to cheer up its budget-conscious guests. American families, conscious of the dollar, and Euro back-packers keep the hotel pretty much booked up in season. Reservations usually essential. Good location for metro connections around the city – but nowhere near the cathedral! Budget 320f per night, breakfast around 30f on top.

RESTAURANTS

➤ Astier
(R)S   *44 r. Jean Pierre Timbaud, 43 57 16 35, V, cl Sat, Sun, Aug, Dec (Parmentier)*

Arrowed for the bon rapport qualité-prix. You won't be able to get a table without booking, since the République quarter is loyal to its favourite dining rooms. Unpretentious, relaxed and joyfully noisy, this is where to go to eat well with friends, especially if you get a table in the front room. The meal costs 130f, and for this you have a long list of savoury first courses, from the obligatory escargots to warm leeks in vinaigrette and marinated anchovies. An equally mouth-watering selection of main courses includes a house favourite – lapin à la moutarde, magret au cidre and a popular andouillette. A massive cheeseboard and a fine choice of substantial desserts round off the good value four courses. The breadth of the menu is matched by an equally rich wine list. Late in 1992, Michel Picard, the patron, whose convivial personality was indelibly stamped on the restaurant, moved on to the Villaret (see below). However, Parisian friends tell me the Astier's quality and style remains unchanged – so the arrow remains.

➤ Chez Fernand/les Fernandises
(R)SM   *17-19 r. de la Fontaine-au-Roi, 43 57 46 25, cl Sun/Mon (Goncourt)*

Take your pick, the informal bistro les Fernandises serves the same carte as the smarter Chez Fernand next door, but the posh address does not have the bistro's bargain lunch menu. I prefer the brown check cloths and garish Commune mural of Les Fernandises – it is more in keeping with the spirit of the food, which is Normand pure and simple. Fernand Asseline prides himself on bringing the spirit and flavours of Normandy to the capital, and this he does. Apart from the standards such as tripes au calvados, confit de canard and so forth, he creates his own dishes with the traditional ingredients of his region. Thus on the day that the markets brought a catch of fresh sea-trout, he produced a sauce of mussels and crème fraîche. I love his deceptively fat-free rillettes de maquereaux, and the simple cream and garlic sauce of the cassoulette of morus. An impressive array of home-cured camemberts with nuts, redcurrants, even cummin is almost a meal on its own, especially with the home-made bread and home-made butter that Gernand's regulars have cherished for years. Desserts range from the crêpes au cidre to apple tart, and despite a pretty fair wine list, with such a regional flavour, can you blame me for choosing cider with my meal? Fernand has a special cider, not on the menu, made in Normandy by his nephew. It has quite a kick, and it is this that he reserves for the kitchen. He also stocks a neat range of Calvados, from a green blow-your-socks-off version, poured straight from the freezer, to a smooth and head-warming 1933 vintage. Service in the bistro is cheery, and prices à la carte in both can come to around the 250f mark. But a four-course menu is a mere 130f, and three courses (bistro lunch only) only 100f. Arrow for country simplicity and good value.

Chez Fernand

Le Villaret
(R)M   13 r. Ternaux, 43 57 89 76, all cc, cl Sun and lunch (Parmentier)

> Early reports on the newest venture by Michel Picard of Astier (see
> above), suggest that 1993's recce might well result in an arrow. The
> good humour of Astier transfers effortlessly with a cheery welcome.
> Picard's respected policy of good value simplicity is reflected on the
> menu. Already, the wild duck with figs and a vanilla crème brulée are
> being spoken of with enthusiasm. The wine cellar is not as vast as at
> Astier. Good news for night owls on the less fashionable Père
> Lachaise side of the République quarter – the restaurant is open
> until 1 am.

Le Repair de Cartouche
(R)M   8 bd. des Filles du Calvaire/99 r. Amelot, 47 00 25 86, all cc, cl Sat lunch,
Sun, Aug (St Sébastian)

> The young team that has taken over this provincial-style restaurant are
> cheerful and welcoming. Brothers Lionel and Emmanuel Salabert have
> established a good reputation for south-western dishes. The warm
> foie gras in cabbage leaves as part of an à la carte meal costing say
> 350f is recommended. However, my experience of the 150f menu is
> less satisfactory. The meal is pleasant enough, but too casual an
> approach is taken in its preparation. An acceptable fish was served
> with overcooked vegetables, and the selection of desserts offered with
> the menu was unimaginative. A set menu should reflect, albeit
> modestly, the style and quality of the house. Here I felt that those of us
> opting for the prix fixe (served weekdays lunch and dinner) were
> regarded by the kitchen at least as second best. A pity because the
> staff are efficient and friendly, and the decor is cosy and attractive. By
> the way if the first address you try seems to be closed, walk around
> the corner and check the second. The double-decker restaurant has
> two entrances, as one road is one storey higher than the other.

Jacques Melac
(R)S   42 r. Léon Frot, 43 70 59 27, cl Sat and Sun (Charonne)

> Wine bars may be thin on the ground in Paris compared to Britain but
> Jacques Melac is everything a wine bar should be. Melac's father set
> the bar up just after World War II. He'd be proud of the result today
> which owes its success to the personality of his son – larger than life,
> usually on parade to meet and greet and put you at ease. If you're in
> Paris in the last week in September and the third Thursday in
> November, book well ahead and join in the grape-squashing
> ceremony (September) and the first Beaujolais Nouveau tasting
> (November). Though most visitors come for the vast range of wines
> (from 70f a glass upwards) omelettes are excellent (cooked runny to
> order) served with home-made breads.

12th ARRONDISSEMENT

(Paris 75012)

It had to happen: 200 years ago the Bastille was stormed by the *sans-culottes.* In our lifetime the area has been taken afresh by the sans soucis – the without-a-care yuppies of the eighties colonised the area that had been contentedly plebeian since the Revolution.

The 12th stretches along the Seine as far as the Bois des Vincennes, the south-eastern woodland park of Paris, but to most Parisians it is the renaissance of the Bastille that gives the district its current high profile.

The glittering new opera house dominates the place itself, even outshining the stunning statue of the Genius of Liberty that features on the new 10f coin. The Arsenal basin, a pleasure port, can be seen from the square and one platform of the tortuous Bastille metro interchange. At night, the square echoes to the sound of motorbikes revving up, and dodgems whirring and crashing – this is very much a young people's rendezvous. The nightclubs of the Bastille are as fashionable with today's youngsters as they once were with their parents.

One, the Balajo, technically in the 11th (see above), has not changed its decor and style since Piaf herself trawled the backstreets with her own bit of rough, fighter Marcel Cerdan, in tow. Even now, as today's young clubbers bop to acid music, the disc jockey will suddenly play a Piaf, Yves Montand or Sinatra record. Monday afternoons, when local traders shut up shop, the Balajo hosts a tea dance for the shopkeepers, who slowdance to accordion sounds.

The warehouses of Bercy, the river-rail freight district, are giving way to some of the most adventurous new architecture in town. The Palais Omnisports with its sloping lawn roofs, and the futuristic bridge-like steel and glass Ministry of Finance building are well worth a visit.

From Bercy to the Bois, the avenue Daumesnil is lined with some excellent restaurants, far enough away from the fashionable end of the arrondissement to provide some very pleasant surprises.

Markets: bd. de Reuilly, Tue, Fri (Daumesnil); Cours des Vincennes, Wed, Sat (Porte de Vincennes); av. Ledru Rollin, Thu, Sat (Gare de Lyon); bd. Poniatowski, Thu, Sun (Porte Dorée); St-Eloi 36-38 r. de Reuilly, Thu, Sun (Reuilly Diderot) – all 7 am-1.30 pm. Covered marché Beauvau St Antoine, r. Aligré (Ledru-Rollin), Tue-Sat 8 am-1 pm, 3.30-7.30 pm, Sun 8 am-1 pm.

HOTELS

Hôtel Claret
(H)M   *44 bd. du Bercy, 46 28 41 31 (Bercy)*

Once upon a time Bercy was known as the wine cellar of Paris. Here were the warehouses for the great wines of France. The Hotel Claret, converted in 1984 from the district's post office, currently standing in the no-man's-land 'twixt the Bercy Motorail station and the futurescape of the Palais Omnisports and Finance Ministry, harks back to the vintage years. Your room key is attached to an enormous cork, and the way to your bedroom is a veritable route des vins. The lift is papered with Bordeaux labels and the corridors are a maze of wine cellars. Each of the 52 rooms is named for a different great wine, and the bottle from the domaine is displayed in a glass case on the wall. The paintings are taken from the etiquette itself. I stayed in Château de

Le Pavillon Bastille

la Petit Thouars; next door was the Domaine of St Aubin de la Poucelle Mersault. Had the hotel not been full, I might have wallowed in Champagne. The motif des vins is continued with the tiling patterns in the cramped bathrooms. The hotel claims almost a dozen styles of decor, from renaissance to art deco. The cheerful reception staff will endeavour to find you a room with decor to suit your taste. To be honest, I found the variety of furnishings less successful than the wine idea. The *coup de grâce* of the theming is that every one of the wines named on a bedroom door may be tasted in the hotel's cellar wine bar. Rooms with bathroom and TV cost around the 400f mark, and those at the front overlook the railway lines.

Le Pavillon Bastille
(H)L   *65 r. de Lyon, 43 43 65 65, all cc (Bastille)*

The sweep of blue and yellow drapes is very much the symbol of this fashionable new address opposite the opera house. A traditional town house, with a computer-key-card front door, this is a quiet address, very much at the heart of a lively quarter of restaurants, culture and nightlife. The stylish decor is summery and attractive. Staffing is discreetly low key, and the smallish rooms very well equipped. Large bathrobes and a fluffy bale of towels make bathtime a leisurely treat. The usual bundle of bathroom freebies is more than matched by a complementary mini-bar included in the 850f per night room rate. Breakfast, served in the basement, is 65f, but generous. In the heat of the summer an air-conditioning unit is parked in a corner of the bedroom. A useful information pack gives the low-down on local shopping, eating and hairdressing. The atmosphere is one of a private house, and guests are encouraged to take the front door key home, to use again on their next visit. Off-peak family rates available for interconnecting rooms, with packages to EuroDisney and the Opera.

La Porte Dorée
(H)S   *273 av. Daumesnil, 43 07 56 97, DC MC V (Porte Dorée)*

This is precisely what a two-star hotel should be: charming, clean and welcoming. The sort of place anxious parents would send their daughter. Half-panelled corridors with painted mirrors, and surprisingly spacious rooms equipped with well tiled, good quality shower and bathrooms. Nothing is too much trouble for Madame and her helpful staff. When I wanted to collect a suitcase at half past midnight, she happily made the arrangements. 28f breakfast is taken either in the bedroom or in one of the two bright morning rooms. With room rates from 250-320f, the Hôtel de la Porte Dorée, on the edge of the Bois de Vincennes and a 20 minute bus ride to the Opéra district, is a bargain.

RESTAURANTS

→**Au Trou Gascon**
(R)ML   *40 r. Taine, 43 44 34 26, all cc, cl weekends (Daumesnil)*

This corner of Gascony is the creation of Alain Dutournier, whose main restaurant, Le Carré des Feuillants in the 1st arrondissement, is the haunt of those who easily part with 600f for dinner. Here, in the less central 12th, Dutournier recalls his Landais childhood. As an introduction to the enormous wine list, he writes of his early influences. In the kitchen, he and Bernard Broux re-create the flavours of the south-west. Eating à la carte (and spending around 400f a head) one can savour the hommard au gazpacho and the pigeonneau sauté a l'ancienne fèves tendres avec leur peau cuisinée au vieux jambon. Or, as I did, relish the 200f lunch menu. I started with a fresh and flavoursome oeuf au pipérade froid, and followed that with saumon aux primeurs – a prime example of the virtue of a restaurant which, although plating each meal most attractively, never regards vegetables as mere garnish or colour. As much attention is paid to their preparation and presentation as to the main attraction. Desserts are choice: my tourtière landaise, served with delicious prune ice-cream was wafer thin, yet heady, and justified my decision to forego cheese for once – though the cabecou looked excellent. The choice of wines is far-ranging; a local south-western accompaniment to the meal would cost 150-300f. In the charming turn of the century dining room, the welcome and service is a practised and relaxed combination of the professional and friendly. One is aware of the quality of the establishment, but never less than relaxed.

Au Pressoir
(R)L   *257 av. Daumesnil, 43 44 38 21, V MC, cl Sat, Sun, Aug (Porte Dorée)*

The Porte Dorée is something of a golden gateway to the tables of the less fashionable end of the 12th. And the avenue Daumesnil alone boasts three (four if you count Trou Gascon) superb dining rooms. Henry Seguin's honey-rich, wood-panelled dining room, with comfortable seats for leaning back and patting the embonpoint in satisfaction, is the setting for painstakingly prepared dishes – at a price. Coeur de filet de boeuf in a truffle coulis served with light fresh pasta, and the legendary pot au feu d'homard are among the delicate mélange of tastes on offer. Desserts are never predictable – peanut ice-cream or banana mousse for example. Pricewise, with the set menu at 370f, and à la carte budget at the 500-600f level, readers might well have to consider their holiday purses before booking.

→**La Gourmandise**
(R)ML   *271 av. Daumesnil, 43 43 94 41, all cc, cl Sun, Mon, Aug (Porte Dorée)*

Good food need not cost the earth. Drink a toast to Alain Denoual and his witty cuisine and cheeky prices. Just 190f for lunch – with a menu express at 140f – mean that a dining room designed for 450f à la carte expense account customers is in the reach of the Entrée gourmet. A roulade of salmon with fresh herbs and vegetables is excellent and the magret de canard aux poivres really works. The wine list is honestly priced, with a good daily selection on the menu at budget prices, such as a Chéverny 1988 at 87f. Sensibly, half bottles are younger vintages than the full bottle as they mature much more quickly. Arrowed for good value lunches. You can walk off the meal in the Bois de Vincennes, just a couple of hundred yards away.

➤ La Sologne
(R)M   *164 av. Daumesnil, 43 07 68 97, V MC, cl Sat lunch, Sun (Daumesnil)*

This is a bistro with a twist. Classic French dishes given a subtle spin by Japanese chef Koji Kaeriyama. Intrigued by the offer of duck à la Japonaise, we discovered the dish to be a faithfully prepared magret de canard, but with an exotic sauce based in soy and oriental seasonings. Kaeriyama's special skill is with fish, however, and the panache des poissons de mer was a delight, served with fresh home-made pasta. Pay around 350f per head, or choose from the modest 175f menu, featuring such dishes as galette de crabe et langoustine à la crème de poireaux. I visited the restaurant in summer, but understand that the year end brings a menu influenced by game, inspired perhaps by the chasse-dominated decor. Staff will patiently explain the more intriguing items on the menu. Arrowed for innovation and imagination.

Le Mange Tout
(R)SM   *24 bd. de la Bastille, 43 43 95 15, AE MC V, cl Sun and end Aug (Bastille)*

When I saw the fashionable yellow of the table linen, alarm bells started to ring. Was this going to be another of those oh so trendy Bastille eateries? I had no need to fear. Under the colours of the branché Parisian chic beats the heart of a south-western foody. Michel Simon had brought the flavours of his region to the tables of the Left Bank for some time, before opening up his new restaurant here opposite the Arsenal Port of the Seine. He strikes the right balance between fashion and simplicity, and brings the riches of south-west France to those who have no wish to leave the table heavy and bloated. My lunch was light and fulfilling. The helpful and efficient waitresses raised no eyebrows when I decided to forego the delicious-sounding main courses and opt for a starter and salad instead. The poached eggs in bleu de causses were precisely the right temperature and texture. For a dairy lover like me, this was the highlight of my day. I followed this with a refreshing salad of smoked salmon on a bed of lettuce and fresh garden herbs. The fish main courses, judging by the appreciative attention being paid to their plates by my neighbours, were obviously a success. If I was awarding points I might quibble about the millefeuille, a tad gooey for my taste. The wine list leans towards Cahors and the Bordelais, and the house wine is what it should be, a good personal choice of the restaurant, rather than dregs from a job lot past its sell by date. The suggested crispy and refreshing young white from the Tarn suited me perfectly. A la carte will come to around 250f, but the menu, available evenings and lunchtimes, for 98f is excellent value. In fact, don't be surprised if you find an arrow on this listing in a future edition of the Entrée.

Le Train Bleu
(R)M *Gare de Lyon, 1st floor, 20 bd. Diderot, 43 43 09 06, all cc, open daily until 10 pm (Gare de Lyon)*

To be visited as a historic rather than a gastronomic monument. This is not your average railway station canteen. Instead it is all your romantic Belle Epoque dreams of the golden age of travel and adventure rolled into one. Towards the end of 1992, the restaurant re-opened after a loving refurbishment, and now it looks even more glorious than when it starred with Maggie Smith in the film *Travels With My Aunt*. Much of Le Train Bleu's sumptuous architecture and paintings remain from its days as a station buffet at the beginning of the century when train travel was a luxury: luxuriant red curtains, extravagant gilts and mirrors, solemn moustached waiters in ankle length starched aprons. Today's restaurant is good by station standards, but don't go expecting a quick 10 minute snack; service is slow and trains don't wait. Stick to simple dishes with simple names. Likewise, try not to stray from the reasonably priced 195f menu; otherwise value is not good.

A la Biche au Bois
(R)S *45 av. Ledru Rollin, 43 43 34 38, MC V AE, cl Sat, Sun, mid-July to mid-Aug, open 12.15-2.30 pm and 7.15-10 pm (Gare de Lyon)*

If food takes precedence over setting when hanging around for trains at the Gare de Lyon, La Biche au Bois is a less attractive, less expensive and, as a result, less pompous alternative to the sumptuous Train Bleu (see above). Outdoors dining in summer, if car fumes and screeching brakes don't bother you. Food is good, interesting and unmessed about: both the terrine of wild boar and fresh salmon served with wood mushrooms were on the excellent value 80f menu; fish is the speciality on Tuesdays and Fridays. Wines equally well priced with a Côtes du Rhône going for 68f.

Fouquets Bastille and Café Fouquets
(R)ML *130 r. de Lyon, 43 42 18 18, V MC AE, cl Sat lunch, Sun (Bastille)*

The opera moved to the Bastille, so the restaurants had to cross town as well. Fouquets (see 8th arrondissement) has always been the haunt of the fashionable, and the main restaurant continues to draw crowds on the Champs Elysées. Its Bastille baby shares the glass cliff face of the opera house, and upstairs produces the goods, with the classic menu favourites. Bills come to the 350f mark. The café with its more basic menu offers, budgetwise, the acceptable face of Fouquets. Seafood and kidney-style bistro fare fill a 165f menu. The restaurant is of course convenient for the Opéra.

13th ARRONDISSEMENT

(Paris 75013)

With the Gare d'Austerlitz offering such a convenient way out of the area, why on earth would anyone want to stay in the 13th arrondissement, or even visit it? That is the unspoken, unkind, but patently heartfelt opinion of some of my more fashionable Parisian acquaintances. On the face of it, they have a point. The Seine border is lined with railway yards, and the bulk of the quarter does seem to be a no-man's-land between the far more interesting 5th arrondissement and the boulevard Périférique.

But take time to explore. The shortage of traditional French restaurants leaves no vacuum. For food, read Chinatown. This is where all Paris goes for a good Chinese, Vietnamese or Thai meal. A growing proportion of the local population hails from the Orient, and that makes for exotic and exciting shopping for the visitor. If you are in Paris around the weekend of the Chinese New Year, you must join in the celebrations around the avenues Ivry and Choisy.

The lack of interesting monuments and sites in the area is compensated for by the warm community spirit, most evident at the Butte aux Cailles, where residents have managed to keep the peculiar styles of their streets, from twenties art deco to pre-war quaint. Remarkable, when you consider the depressing square blocks of flats covering almost all the rest of the quarter. Visit the studios of local artisans, including the tapestry workshops of Les Gobelins.

Markets: r. Bobillot, Tue, Fri (Tolbiac); bd. Vincent Auriol, Wed, Sat (Nationale); bd. Auguste Blanqui, Tue, Fri, Sun (Corvissart); Maison Blanche, 186 ave. d'Italie, Thu, Sun (Maison Blanche), Hôpital Salpêtrière, Tue, Fri (St Marcel) pl. Jeanne d'Arc, Thu, Sun (Nationale). All 7 am-1.30 pm.

HOTELS

➤**Résidence des Gobelins**
H(M)   *9 r. des Gobelins, 47 07 26 90, all cc (Les Gobelins)*

A living example of the importance of that good old-fashioned and increasingly rare concept called Welcome. What the Residence des Gobelins lacks in interior decor, it more than compensates for in its genuine warm 'accueil' – hence its much deserved arrow. Well-priced bearing in mind its central location in the heart of this fascinating 15th-century quarter close to rue Mouffetard and the old Gobelin cloth factory. Less than 400f buys you a sparkling clean and comfy, well-equipped, though not particularly memorable double room. Owners Philippe Poirier – a French architect in his spare time – and Californian wife Jennifer (English therefore no problem) go out of their way to welcome, chat and spoil, disappearing just when the time's right. Substantial breakfasts served in their pretty garden in summer or in the flowery dining room: 30f for a generous selection of cereals, yoghurts, breads and fresh fruit juices (clearly the American influence versus the French).

Verlaine
(H)S *51r. Bobillot, 45 89 56 14, MC V (place d'Italie)*

The Fontaine family run a modest little hotel where around 300f buys a double room with bath, 270f for a room with shower. Standard breakfast for 26f. Bring a swimsuit because next door is the historic municipal swimming baths where medical breakthroughs in therapeutic swimming were made during the last war. Pool charges are just 10f.

RESTAURANTS

L'Omelet'rit
(R)SM *20 r. de la Procidence, 45 89 99 27, MC V (Corvissart)*

Finding a French restaurant in the 13th is not as simple as it seems. This is the quarter where Parisians, tired of magret de canard and tête du veau, come for their exotic Chinese and Vietnamese restaurants. They also find standard brasserie fare around the modern multi-screen cinemas of the place d'Italie, and there are any number of bar-restos near the street market on the boulevard Blanqui. Still, on our way to a quite different table we passed L'Omelet'rit, run by Michel, who caters for functions and private parties. And the selection of six different menus for such a tiny little restaurant caught my eye. So we stayed for lunch. Bright modern decor kept spotlessly clean, with fresh lemon roses on the table. Menus at 85f, 110f, 135f and 185f are thoughtfully chosen and very tempting at all price ranges. There is a diététique menu at 165f including freshly squeezed grapefruit juice and a midweek omelette-based lunch deal at 60f. Pay an expensive 250f à la carte. We opted for the 135f, which included a blackberry kir, and when, on a whim, I asked for a trou normand, the waiter flourished a massive Calvados sorbet between courses (charging me just 28f extra). A feuilleté of escargots made a warming starter. Despite the meat base of the main menu, fish is deftly handled as well. A savoury salad of chèvre with walnuts had an offbeat and piquant dressing of crème fraîche with raspberry vinegar. The kitchen is visible from most tables in the dining room and the chef's skill with his reassuringly battered battery of coppers and skilletts is entertaining. The youngish wine list is serviceable and averagely priced.

L'Espérance
(R)S *9 r. de l'Espérance, 45 80 22 55, no cc (Corvisart)*

No frills, but a nourishing meal for less than 50f, including wine. The 47f menu includes faux-filet and rabbit pâté with a quarter bottle of wine or a demi-pression of beer. This is a typical neighbourhood bar, which serves a solid basic lunch and dinner – even on a Sunday, when diners can sniff out the heady scents of the nearby street markets to work up an appetite.

14th ARRONDISSEMENT

(Paris 75014)

A wedge from Montparnasse to the Périférique, the 14th is for the most part an inner city suburb, happily self-sufficient and, in the southern section of Alésia and Porte d'Orléans, very little to do with Paris. Even British newspapers take an extra day to reach the news stands.

Around Montparnasse, however, all is cosmopolitan and Parisian, with a touch of good manners thrown in. Walking back to the hotel late one night, a friend and I approached a threatening-looking gang of bikers. As we passed them, they chorused politely ''soir monsieur-dame'. At la Coupole, night-people gossip the small hours away with a coffee or brasserie blow-out. This and a handful of other venues created the Café Society that was Paris for the first half of this century.

The intellectuals no longer pack the tables of the Coupole and the Dôme. Instead they rest in peace at the Montparnasse cemetery where Baudelaire, Sartre and de Beauvoir are amongst the famous residents.

Less illustrious former Parisians are filed, with disturbing efficiency, in the caves and crannies of the catacombs. Post-Revolutionary zeal led to the subterranean network of Roman passageways being called into service as an ordered ossuary. The putrid cemeteries of the cities were emptied and re-landscaped, with the thighs and skulls of the previous tenants being removed to the catacombs.

The wartime Underground lived up to their name, using the passageways as a secret HQ during the war. Today a short route through the bones and stones is open to visitors at Denfert-Rochereau.

The Montparnasse area is named after the home of the gods – and the tower, that guides all rive gauche navigation, pierces the heavens at the crossroads of four arrondissements.

With the great TGV station at its foot, and bus shuttles to Orly Airport, this is the southern equivalent of the Gare du Nord-dominated 10th arrondissement. Just a short step from the station is the rue de la Gaité where merry-making is assured. Theatres, night-clubs and restaurants give the street the nickname of the West End of the 14th.

The south of the district, Alésia–Porte d'Orléans, is the most residential section. Butchers, supermarkets and auction rooms line the streets. Cinemas show dubbed versions of the Hollywood blockbusters, screened with subtitles on the Champs Elysées. Local restaurants feed local people, too tired to cook after a hard day at the office.

Don't be misled. This sleepy quarter boasts at least two gastronomic giants amongst its chefs. And not all the residents have been contented stay-at-homes: 4 rue Marie Rose was the home of Lenin before the Revolution. His lively chats with house-guest Trotsky may have raised a few eyebrows at the local bars and cafés.

Between Alésia and the city limits is the Park Montsouris, where an afternoon watching the swans makes for good battery re-charging.

> Markets: r. d'Alésia, Wed, Sat (Glacière); bd. Brune, Thu, Sun (Porte de Vances); bd. Edgar Quinet, Wed, Sat (Edgar Quinet); Montrouge, Mouton-Duvernet, Tue, Fri (Mouton Duvernet); av. Villemain, Wed, Sun (Plaisance). All 1 am-1.30 pm. Fleamarket at Porte de Vanves, Sat, Sun (Porte de Vanves) 7 am-7.30 pm.

HOTELS

Châtillon
(H)S   11 sq. du Châtillon, 45 42 31 17, V MC (Alésia)

Not in a square, as such, but a quiet side street off the avenue Jean Moulin in the residential Alésia district, the Châtillon is reliable, welcoming, clean and simple. M. et Mme Lamouret, the owners, are stylish and cheerful, and they keep an immaculate house. No-nonsense old-fashioned bathrooms adjoin basically furnished rooms that are a good size for the mere 300f charged. Breakfast, at 28f, is a sociable affair where guests are treated as named individuals on holiday, rather than packages for processing through the tourist mill.

La Loire
(H)S   39 bis r. du Moulin Vert, 45 40 66 88, MC V (Alésia)

This isn't really a Paris hotel at all, it is one of those simple little lodgings one finds when motoring through rural France. It must have been transplanted to this quiet side street off the aptly named rue des Plantes. Mme Noel might suggest one of the small ground floor rooms facing the sweet little garden. If they are all taken, then accept a first floor room overlooking the trees, shrubs and clay tiles. Like the bedrooms, bathrooms are basic with small towels. Breakfast is taken either in the room or around the large family dining table in the reception, where guests are introduced over coffee and baguettes. Budget around 300f a night, 27f for breakfast.

RESTAURANTS

→ La Cagouille
(R)M   10 pl. Brancusi, 43 22 09 01, MC V, cl Sun, Mon, most Aug (Gaité)

Don't be put off by the decor. The brash blues and sea shell and chandlery displays might be naff even for a port – but take my word for it – despite the interior design and the bright shirts of the waiters, this is touted as one of the finest fish restaurants in the city. In the unlikeliest of up-and-coming areas, in the very shadow of Paris' innovative public housing projects, the bright and open Cagouille attracts an intriguing mix of foodies, business types and Government ministers with their mistresses. The menus are scribbled on large white boards erected at your table, and first courses are advised for the hungry, because the service is so slow that even the generous bowl of seafood served as an appetizer will not last until the main course comes. A refreshing summer salad of smoked haddock and spinach is delicious, and the main courses reflect the style of Gérard Allemandou, the acclaimed chef. Salmon and tuna are accorded the same respect due to charolais beef, so be prepared to order à l'unilatérale but lightly flamed on one side, and raw at its heart. Wine is served by the glass from around 25f for a Muscadet; expect to pay 250f for your meal during the day and anything from 350f in the evenings. Reservations are essential, and even then may not guarantee a coveted seat by the window in summer. An arrow for providing the standards of the port in the landlocked 14th.

➤ **La Régalade**
(R)SM   49 av. Jean Moulin, 45 45 68 58, MC V, cl Sat lunch, Mon (Alésia)

If a visitor ever needed an excuse to stay in this dormitory district of Alésia, then the Régalade, hardly known outside the arrondissement, is it. Yves Camdeborde, formerly number two at the Hôtel Crillon, has created a little gem. In this unpretentious but pretty dining room, with its centrepiece of crusty loaves, is served an imaginative and memorable meal to satisfy the palate and the wallet. The menu is 150f for three courses – although a seasonal dégustation may be prepared to suit specific parties – and a shrewd, predominantly young, wine list includes at least a dozen creditable offerings under 100f. Eschewing the foppish fancies offered elsewhere as amuse-gueules, La Régalade puts at the diner's disposition a large earthenware pot – the house terrine du porc – with an excalibur knife plunged at its heart. Do not yield to temptation. The brunch nature of the appetizer belies the finesse of the cuisine that follows, so keep the taste buds on hold. A terrine de poireaux et queues de boeuf au vin rouge is something quite different. And as for the pisaladière de thon mi-cuit aux olives noires, just imagine the wafers of subtly heated tuna on the crispest fine pastry base, topped with a nest of fresh herbs. A revelation. The hachis Parmentier of boudin noir béarnaise and dos de carralet that followed were masterly improvements on the traditional servings, the latter bearing no relation to the bland offering of many Paris restaurants, served here on a bed of warm and crispy white cabbage and chives. The triumphant soufflé finale only served to underline the award of an arrow for value, flavour, and imagination. As word of mouth and recommendation gathers momentum, I trust that success will not spoil this unexpected treasure.

Aux Iles Marquises
(R)SM   15 r. de la Gaité, 43 20 93 58, AE MC V, cl Sat, Sun, end Aug (Edgar Quinet)

Don't come as a pilgrim in search of les années Piaf. The chanteuse and her boxing and showbusiness crowd would not recognise the place since modernisation. With decor that practically turns the bar into a trawler and the entire façade of the building painted salmon pink, no prizes for guessing that seafood is still a speciality, under the new chef-proprietor Mathieus Théry, and jolly good stuff too. My guest plunged enthusiastically into the prawns, while I played safe with salads. My weakness is for the delicious desserts. A la carte comes to around 400f, if one raids the wine cellar, but there is a choice of menu under 200f.

Moulin Vert

Au Moulin Vert
(R)S   *34 bis r. des Plantes, 45 39 31 31, V MC (Alésia)*

A veritable rainforest of lush vegetation sprouts on the corner of the rue Moulin Vert and the aptly named rue des Plantes, parting at the entrance to this cheery green and pink restaurant. Big and bustling, it has the eighties decor and efficient staff of a boulevard brasserie-restaurant in the touristic south, though the clientele seems to come mainly from the residents of this very domestic quarter. The fare is acceptably good; no gastronomic surprises, but a varied menu offers excellent value for the price – 170f for three courses, including apéritif, wine and coffee – and no extras to boost the bill. A tartare of haddock and salmon served with poached egg made a suitable first course, and we had no complaints about the faux fillet and truite de mer that followed. This is the place for a cheerful evening out after a day spent traipsing round the shops and museums of central Paris.

Rendez-vous des Camionneurs
(R)S   *34 r. des Plantes, 45 40 43 36, cl weekends and Aug (Alésia)*

Buff up those tattoos for a red-blooded meat supper. Actually you would not be able to park a lorry in this street, so your actual camionneurs are somewhat thin on the ground. But the locals know a bargain when they see one, and a 60f menu of wedges of country pâté and solid steak served until 9 pm, brings the budget conscious to this cheery bistro.

Natacha
(R)M   *17 bis r. Campagne Première, 43 20 79 27, V MC AE, cl Sun, end Aug (Raspail)*

Play spot the movie star, then pay like a movie star chez Natacha, who herself greets the regulars or celebrities, so that we mere mortals know exactly which supermodel or Polanski-bride is which. The food is acceptable – but for 300f you are paying to gawp not to guzzle – and the variations on traditional recipes, such as hachis Parmentier, are the best bet. The main topic of conversation amongst those of us who are not here to discuss our latest film deal, is how on earth these people manage to keep their figures after eating Natacha's creamy and calorie packed desserts.

Le Bar à Huîtres
(R)M   *112 bd. du Montparnasse, 43 20 71 01, V MC AE (Vavin)*

Remember that film where Gene Kelly, Phil Silvers and was it Rita Hayworth used to spend the midnight hours sitting at a New York bar cracking 'ersters' in search of the natural jewel that would make their fortune. You can do the same here with the late night Montparnasse crowd. Stay at the bar until 2 in the morning and choose from as fine a range of Breton beauties as ever hid a pearl. The dining room has an excellent sea-borne carte including traditional salt cod dishes and the inevitable fruits de mer. At the table spend around 250-300f including wine.

Théâtre Montparnasse
(R)S   *31 r. de la Gaité, 43 22 77 74, open Tue-Fri from 7 pm, Sat from 8 pm (Gaité)*

Oh, la rue de la Gaité. This little Montparnasse street has six theatres, the academy of Commedia dell'Arte and the Bobino, where Josephine Baker gave her final performance. It has its cafés, brasseries, burlesque revues and sex shops and is every bit as naughty as Paris is supposed to be. Happily, all attempts to clean up the Gaité and turn it into the respectable 'West End' of the 14th have so far failed, and the Gaité retains its raffish charm. The beautiful Théâtre Montparnasse, on a street corner, is a 19th century gem. Great stars such as Zizi Jeanmaire can be seen here, and artistes join theatregoers and locals squeezing into the little street café in a corner of the foyer. One of the old style bars with a rack of hard-boiled eggs on the counter, has a charm of its own, but if you want to eat before the show, the dress circle on the first floor of the theatre does a nice line in brasserie cuisine. Chunks of cold pâté or hot dishes such as navarin d'agneau with seasonal vegetables taken with dessert and a glass of wine or beer will set you back no more than 100f.

Théâtre Montparnasse

La Perle des Antilles
(R)SM   *36 av. Jean Moulin, 45 42 91 25, all cc, cl Sun (Alésia)*

A welcome and a repast from Haiti awaits in the simply painted
whicker-furnished restaurant. Snack lunches – including wine – from
59f and full menus from just over 100f offer value and a taste of the
exotic. A la carte comes to around 220f. Service is warm and smiling.

Istria
(H)M   *29 r. Campagne Première, 43 20 91 82 (Raspail, Port Royal or RER Denfert-
Rochereau)*

Rue Campagne Première is artist territory – vestiges of the glorious
thirties era remain behind every door. And little has changed since at
the Istria where surrealists once flocked (Miller, Walter Benjamin and
Co) to wine, dine and rest. Sadly, parts of the hotel have been over-
modernised and tidied up. But rooms are comfy with all mod cons,
each one bearing clues of this area's interesting photographic and
artistic heritage. Monsieur and Madame Leroux, our charming hosts,
have many a story to relate on past visitors. Go for rooms overlooking
the patio for peace and quiet. Prices are pretty standard for the area –
470-520f for a double, with breakfast (served in a pretty, vaulted cellar)
for 35f.

Le Cabanon des Maîtres Nageurs
(R)SM   *9 r. Léopold Robert, 43 20 61 14, cl Sat, Sun and Mon lunch (Raspail)*

Even before the meal arrives, you're halfway to Corsica, the homeland
of the very friendly, very robust owner, Bernard, who has created a
throughly Mediterranean atmosphere in this unpretentious little
restaurant. Woodwork and beach photos set the scene. Starters are
usually a selection of delectable charcuteries and cured hams. To
follow, roast kid or, perhaps more typical, cod 'à la Corse' cooked with
tomatoes, potatoes and olive oil. Go for cheese if you like it strong,
keeping room for a salad of orange and grapefruit in a sharp caramel
sauce. At lunchtime you can get away with a 100f note two courser
with wine; otherwise bank on 250f.

Pavillon du Parc Montsouris
(R)M   *20 r. Gazan, DC V, open all year 12.15-2.30 pm and 7.45-10.30 pm (RER Cité
Université)*

In the centre of this beautiful 16 hectare English-style country park is
an eccentric little pavilion built in Napoleon III's days. Many a celebrity
has dined here (Sartre and Lenin were regulars) and for the romanticly
inclined, there could be no setting more perfect for that starlit post-
meal promenade. Inside, all is extravagant and Hollywood-style – pink
seats, pink materials, pink chandeliers … But most customers come

for the surroundings (romantic) and the cuisine (innovative and reliable), though the connoisseur might find some dishes a bit over the top. My succulent ravioli stuffed with langoustines were sublime, likewise the dessert of baked white peaches filled with home-made vanilla ice-cream. Good value for a 250f menu, but the wines can up the prices substantially – 270f for a Chablis was pushing it.

15th ARRONDISSEMENT

(Paris 75015)

Despite having the towering twin sirens of Eiffel and Montparnasse luring helpless visitors to its borders, the rest of the 15th arrondissement, sprawling towards the périphérique, offers little of interest to the tourist. A jaded executive staying at the Paris Hilton, can expect little more than a pleasant stroll along the Seine.

Leisure hours can be spent in the new Parc Georges Brassens, with its highly-scented garden for the blind, or luxuriating on the tropical beaches of Aquaboulevard – a swimming-pool theme-park, with tennis and golf among the drier attractions.

One of the three Statues of Liberty is to be found on the riverbank. Another is in the Jardins de Luxembourg. The third is somewhere in America, I believe.

Markets: Cervantes, r. Bargue, Wed (Volontaires); r. de la Convention, Tue, Thu, Sun (Convention); bd. de Grenelle, Wed, Sun (Dupleix); r. St Charles, Tue, Fri (Charles Michels); r. Lecourbe, Wed, Sat (Balard); bd. Lefèbvre, Wed, Sat (Porte de Versailles). All 7 am-1.30 pm.

HOTELS

Lecourbe
(H)M   *28 r. Lecourbe, 47 34 49 06, (Sèvres-Lecourbe or Pasteur)*

Family-run and friendly, clean, comfortable and cheap for its location just 10 minutes from Montparnasse. Worthwhile forking out those extra francs for one of the suites at the end of the courtyard where rooms are not only larger, but lack the constant noise of traffic on the busy rue Lacourbe which plagues the front rooms. The welcome is professional and sober, likewise the decor with pastel shades the norm. Substantial buffet breakfasts are served in the central patio in summer. Rooms range from 400-540f for a double, 350f for a single.

RESTAURANTS

➤**Le Clos Morillons**
(R)M *50 r. des Morillons, 48 28 04 37, V MC, cl Sat lunch, Sun, Aug (Convention)*

From the outside, the burgundy frontage seems little more than a conventional bistro. Inside all is clean, modern, subtly tropical in style – and most definitely a restaurant. Courteous staff serve excellent food. Poached egg with wild mushrooms in a chive dressing is superb. Veal cooked with thyme and puréed almonds is fine, and the fish is accorded the respect of a port restaurant. Tuna steak is served on a bed of courgette, with pieces of lemon to cut through any richness of the butter sauce; salmon is almost unilatérale with crisply toasted skin, and silken rare meat. And the desserts are a revelation. As well as the smoothest of crèmes brulées and a papillotte of figs and grapes caramelised in honey, comes an entire section of the menu devoted to dark chocolate specialists. The gâteau scented with jasmine, the crispy confection of cocoa and praline, quenelles of dark chocolate – all testament to chef-patron Pierre Delacourcelle's pâtissier days at Fauchon (see 8th arrondissement). Wines are well chosen and include gems from the Loire. The carte-menu is just 230f, excellent value. A special set menu is offered at 160f, and for 285f the restaurant has a six course Menu Découverte. The Discovery is heightened (for a 60f supplement) with a different wine for each course. Arrowed for quality value for money.

Olympe
(R)M *8 r. Nicholas Charlet, 45 31 91 91, V MC, cl Sat, Sun and one month from 14 July (Pasteur)*

A surprisingly spicy amuse-gueule is a mistake. The fashionable appetizer is intended to prepare the palate rather than anaesthetise the mouth. Nonetheless, what follows is worthy of the restaurant's reputation. Dated claret decor is disarming in a fashionable venue, and the warmth of the welcome, and chatty candour of the staff sets up the relaxing mood for the good food to come. Albert Nahmias has created a two-tier menu, offering trendy restaurant dishes alongside excellent bistro fare. Menus from 160f-285f. With some honourable exceptions – such as the braised merlon in saffron butter (a cholesterol booster if ever I tasted one) – the rich menu owes much to the farmyard and field (raviolis de canard au jus among the specialities). Desserts include a scrummy Paris-Brest, that gooey choux confection packed with praline cream. A decanter of house wine on the table helps cut through the richness of much of the meal's sauces. Single diners are not shunted behind coat racks, but welcomed into the fold. For private chats the round tables in the centre of the room escape the eavesdropping that is much of the charm of the rest of the restaurant. People do talk here – the place buzzes at lunchtime and murmurs by night.

L'Oie Cendrée
(R)SM   *51 r. Labrouste, 45 31 91 91, MC V, cl Sat, Sun, month from July 14 (Plaisance)*

Two charming, if low-key, little rooms in which to enjoy a simple selection of south-western farmyard specialities, prepared by Olivier Andreys. Goose and duck dominate the modest menus – the cheaper 95f menu, served until 9 pm, and the second at 125f. The limited wine list includes acceptable Bergerac and Cahors at under 80f and a Graves at 90f.

Café du Commerce
(R)S   *51 r. du Commerce, 45 75 03 27 (la Motte Piquet)*

A long-time haunt of students, budgeting tourists and locals of the 15th arrondissement. However much you indulge, it's hard to spend over 100f on a simple and satisfying lunch or dinner. Even the 1963 *Guide Bleu* on Paris cited the Commerce as one of the capital's best when it comes to quality versus price. Decor is fun, bordering on the kitsch. For 100f you can choose from a daily-changing menu – escargots, steak au poivre, cassoulet, all good honest grub.

Le Serin
(R)SM   *1 pl. Falguière, 47 34 12 24, all cc (Voluntaires)*

The Vidal family provide a warm welcome to their very auberge-style, visitor-friendly restaurant. Animal hide, chalet lanterns and lots of wood set the style for strongly flavoured and sauced dishes – a cassoulette de poisson dowsed in saffron and the usual casseroles. Menus at 120f and 165f.

16th ARRONDISSEMENT

(Paris 75016)

The 16th arrondissement from the Seine to the Bois de Boulogne has a grand imperial gateway – the Arc de Triomphe. The Bois itself is practically a region in its own right, with the excellent restaurants, racecourses and the night-time no-go areas.

The imposing Palais de Chaillot at Trocadéro, with its museums and theatres, offers an unrivalled view of the Champs de Mars and the Eiffel Tower.

Chaillot's Museum of French monuments is an indoor Tour de France, and the Henri Laglois museum of cinema is supported by the impressive cinemathèque. The modern art museum at the Palais de Tokyo has courted controversy for more than half a century.

Nonetheless, in the main, this is but a wealthy dormitory with little to do in the evenings. If one is a non-resident or unable to afford the higher restaurant prices, the 16th can seem cold and unwelcome. The icy personality cracks slightly at year's end, when France's great touring circuses pitch their tents near the périphérique. For the rest of the year, this remains a district of closed doors.

Marché bd. Amiral-Bruix, Wed, Sat (Porte Maillot); Auteuil, rues Auteil, Donizetti and la Fontaine, Wed, Sat (Michelange Auteuil); rues Gros and La Fontaine, Tue, Fri (Jasmin); av. Président Wilson, Wed, Sat (Léna); Porte Molitor, Tue, Fri (Porte d'Auteuil); Point de Jour, av. de Versailles, Tue, Thu, Sun (Porte de St Cloud). All 7 am-1.30 pm. Covered markets: Passy, r. Bois-le-Vent (La Muette) and r. St Didier (Victor Hugo) both Tue-Sat, 8 am-1 pm, 4-7.30 pm and Sun 8 am-1 pm.

HOTELS

St James Paris
(H)L   *5 pl. du Chancelier Adenauer, 47 04 29 29, all cc (Porte Dauphine)*

Once the St James Club, now a hotel, this is a city centre château between the Bois and the Arc de Triomphe. We savoured the luxury of château living, and strolled along to the Champs Elysées to catch the midnight show at the Lido. Away from the bright lights we lounged in the library bar supping the Paris Pimms, an exclusive cocktail

St James Paris

prepared by Marty, the English barman, who accompanied the French Olympic Team to Korea. Staff outnumber guests two to one – but at around 2,000f a night for a room, and far more for a suite, that's to be expected. Rooms and suites are very well equipped, two phone lines into each, the duplexes having phones upstairs and downstairs, and an extra receiver in the spacious marbled bathrooms. Fruit, flowers and drinks are waiting in the rooms. Some of the suites have conservatories, and there are gatehouse pavillons as well for privacy at a price.

Villa Maillot
(H)L   *143 av. de Malakoff, 45 01 25 22, all cc (Porte Maillot)*

Sierra Leone's loss is our gain. The one time embassy is a haven amongst the business blocks of the Porte Maillot conference district. This is restored art deco at its expensively comfortable best. Pink marble bathrooms, comfortable bedrooms and very stylish lounges make it a choice of those who cheerfully part with 1,600f a night for a pampered respite from meetings. The hotel restaurant **Le Jardin** (closed weekends and August) has a pretty floral courtyard where fresh fish dishes are served in the traditional manner: grilled, meunière and en papillote. A la carte dining for around 350f.

Du Bois
(H)M   *11 r. du Dôme, 45 00 31 96, MC V AE (Etoile)*

Cheery welcome, clean redecorated bedrooms and a manageable room rate of around 460f, make this a popular choice for Brits who need to be at the centre of things near the Etoile, but have no intention of paying Champs Elysées prices. Near the fashion houses and posh frocks of the Victor Hugo district, you can lose the extra inches required for that Balmain or Dior original by climbing the stairs to bed – there is no lift!

RESTAURANTS

→Caveau des Echanssons
(R)S   *r. des Eaux, 45 25 63 26, open 12 noon-6 pm (Passy)*

The Caveau des Echanssons is just what its name says it is – the wine waiters' cellar. What better place to sample France's favourite drink than in the capital's wine museum. The cellars were renovated after their World War II function as air raid shelters. In 1984 the Bacchus Brotherhood of French Wine Waiters took over, working for 'the defence and propaganda of French wines' so their slogan goes. Decor is simple, meals are taken under the impressive stone vaults which originate from the 14th century Abbaye de Passy. Food is not the main reason for coming here so stick to simple dishes – perhaps a selection of cheeses and charcuterie to complement the vast range of very well-priced wines on offer.

➤ Faugeron
(R)L   *52 r. de Longchamp, 47 04 24 53, MC V, cl Sat, Sun, Aug, Xmas (Trocadéro)*

Good food requires good wine, and the definitive list here is prepared by Jean-Claude Jambon, voted in 1986 as the world's leading sommelier. In the honeyed-oak dining room spend time browsing through the list and the menu. And what a menu. The croustillant de ris de veau au jus de truffes may be the highlight, but what of the smoothest of soft boiled eggs cossetted by puréed truffle. When game is in season, prepare to be surprised by a potent combination of traditional recipes with Henri Faugeron's ever-revelatory touch: a fruity presentation of saddle of hare, guinea-fowl en cocotte. Desserts are as heady as the main course, from chocolate soufflé to the unmatchable apple Charlotte. From the moment the doorman welcomes you to the light and luxurious restaurant to the presentation of the bill (lunch menu 320f, evenings 550f wine included, and around 700f à la carte), attention to service and cuisine is second to none.

La Grande Cascade
(R)L   *Bois de Boulogne, 45 27 33 51, all cc, cl Christmas, end Jan*

When money is no object, then the Belle Epoque style of the Grande Cascade is definitely *the* place for intimate evenings à deux – that's what everyone else is here for and who can blame them. Immortalised in countless love stories, that theatrical façade is the most exciting of the various restaurants in the park – the gateway to romance. Mere mortals with an eye on the budget may settle for a lunch menu at under 300f. Located in the beautiful Bois de Boulogne, this is where seductions and proposals take place in the movies. On a spring or midsummer's night, there's many an opportunity for pre- or post-meal preambles. Outdoors terrace dining in summer, surrounded by flowers and birds. Service is attentive and discreet. Menus change daily. Watch out for overly rich sauces and concentrate on the first two courses, such as the excellent sea bream or the reliable rognons de veau. Desserts are a let down. Allow 600f per person, especially if you are planning a foray into the endless wine cellar.

Brasserie le Coq
(R)M   *2 pl. du Trocadéro, 47 27 89 52, open all year (Trocadéro)*

Play dodge the newscaster and escape the skateboards on the world's most photographed terrace at Chaillot. It is here that journalists file their reports to camera with Gustave Eiffel's mecano monument over the left shoulder; and here that breakdancers, roller-skaters and buskers weave around the Kodak-clicking masses. Then eat. Brasserie fare reliably served until after midnight, at unbrasserie prices more geared to business accounts than the locals. Good fresh seafood dishes, a respectable steak tartare and other classics do not disappoint. A la carte will come to around 200f. Perhaps because of the constant media circus at the Troc, a figure-conscious menu at 139f offers three courses for less than 700 calories.

Brasserie de la Poste
(R)M   *54 r. de Longchamp, 47 55 01 31, V MC AE (Trocadéro)*

Those who cannot afford a regular date at Faugeron next door, can still join the fashionable monde of BCBG Parisian yuppies. Pieds de porc and cassoulet at under 100f are not over-cheap, but won't break the bank. And the 16th has never been the bargain basement of the capital. Go for the classics such as moules marinières or soups if you fancy a budget lunch, otherwise hand over a 200f note. Wine is served by the glass, and is surprisingly good value. Open until 1 am it is a late night rarity in the pricey Trocadéro district.

17th ARRONDISSEMENT

(Paris 75017)

The railway sidings and yards of Clichy and Batignolles dominate a district that spans the Arc de Triomphe and Montmartre. Like other inexpensive areas, it has been discovered by restaurateurs who are venturing away from the corner of the place de l'Etoile and opening up in the unlikeliest streets.

This means realistic prices for good food, and opportunities for talented young chefs to experiment and develop away from the scrutiny of the critics.

Marché bd. Berthier, Wed, Sat (Péreire); r. Navier, Tue, Fri (Porte de St Ouen). Both 7 am-1.30 pm. Covered markets: Batignolles, r. Lemercier (Brochant) Tue-Sat 8 am-1 pm and 4-7.30 pm, Sun 8 am-12.30 pm; and Ternes, r. Lebon (Ternes) Tue-Sat 8 am-1 pm, 3.30-7.30 pm, Sun 8 am-1 pm. Flower market: pl. des Ternes, Tue-Sun (Ternes) 8 am-7.30 pm.

HOTELS

➤**Hôtel de Banville**
(H)L   *166 bd. Berthier, 42 67 70 16 (Porte de Champerret or Péreire)*

Mademoiselle Lambert is the third generation of Lamberts to run this very special little hotel. If central location is not priority than the Hôtel de Banville has the lot. Value for money (600f for a double), warm family atmosphere and best of all the decor. Outside, in a pretty plane-tree lined avenue, is a classic art deco façade. Inside, all is stylish and refined with the house's older features carefully and lovingly preserved – the old-fashioned lift, the elegant bannister, complemented by a tasteful selection of fabrics and tapestries throughout. Gentle background music rounds off the scene nicely.

Sunshine pours in through the boulevard-side bedrooms; rooms on the other side are darker, but also quieter; all are equipped with the usual mod cons. Three types of breakfast are served, a welcome change from the standard coffee and croissant, including one for dieters. An arrow for the good welcome, good value and charm.

Les Trois Coronnes
(H)M *30 r. de l'Arc de Triomphe, 43 80 46 81, all cc (Etoile)*

Monsieur Lafont presides over the reception desk of his hotel in the fashion of the convivial host of a left bank café. Unsurprising when you learn that until eight years ago that was exactly what he did. His move from bar patron to hotelier brings a touch of left bank informality to the often prissy Etoile. The Lafonts care nothing for fashionable hotel design. They know what they like, and decorate to their own tastes – an eccentric mix of deco and nouveau for the foyer, hand-painted motifs on doors and rough and ready hessian walls in the bedrooms. Pay around 550f for a room with mini-bar and bath. 30f for basic breakfast.

Tilsitt Etoile
(H)M *23 r. Brey, 43 80 39 71, all cc (Etoile)*

Modernised rooms look out on a cleverly mirrored courtyard garden. Simple decor, with bright modern pictures on the walls make it popular with American and Scandinavian visitors. A cheerful bar in the foyer is a meeting point for guests. 660f per room is not cheap. Breakfast at 45f is served in a bright and spacious room. Mme Cot continues to welcome and advise her guests as she has for the past 30 years.

Hôtel Chéverny
(H)M *7 Villa Berthier, 43 80 46 42 (Porte de Champerret or Péreire)*

Standard, 'functional' hotel – convenient for the bus to Roissy airport and for whenever the nearby Hôtel de Banville is full. Clean, comfortable, but characterless rooms sometimes verging on the small. Reasonably priced (around 500f for a double, 440f for a single).

Hotel Regent's Garden
(H)L *6 r. Pierre Demours, 45 74 07 30 (Ternes or Etoile)*

Once inside the picture-book garden of this elegant residence, it's hard to believe the screeching brakes and car fumes of the Etoile are just a stone's throw away. Potential for an arrow is there – spacious, light, airy rooms, high ceilings, impressive marble fireplaces and intricate architectural features from the Napoleon III period. Sadly the existing decor does not do the building's architecture any favours – colours and patterns are heavy and over the top. Full marks, however, for comfort (mini-bars, hair-driers and TV in all rooms) and location (seventy of Paris' top restaurants are within a 150m radius). Most rooms overlook the garden (good for breakfast dining in summer); the two ground floor rooms are the most spacious. Double rooms go for anything between 580f and 880f with breakfast an additional 34f.

RESTAURANTS

➤**Iwi des Mers**
(R)S   *74 r. Jouffroy, 42 27 09 11, V (Villiers)*

An arrow goes to this innovative little restaurant for its attempts (long-lasting let's hope) at offering interesting fish dishes (its speciality as the restaurant's name implies) at interesting prices. Menus change daily according to what's best in the market, but whatever the variety, everything is served imaginatively and generously. Clientele are young, trendy – lots of career women dining on diet menus. Both the 3-course 60f lunch and 80f dinner menus are simple, yet sufficient with fish featuring heavily. Further branches are expected to open soon, all sticking to the successful formula of value and quality.

La Cloche au Fromage
(R)M   *71 bd. Gouvion Saint Cyr, 45 72 50 06, CB (Porte Maillot)*

A must for cheese fans. Seventy varieties to choose from in all shapes, smells and sizes. Take it in a fondue, raclette or soup or best of all cooked to melting point inside a baked apple. If the decision's just too much, go for a 'dégustation' of as many as you like. Wines are served cheaply by the pitcher. Service is young, friendly and relaxed, likewise the average customer. Spend under 200f for a filling, cholesterol-packed meal.

Caves Pétrissans
(R)S   *30 av. Niel, 42 27 82 84 (Ternes)*

Full marks to Tristan Bernard whose wine bar is a successful (and unusual) combination of bar, restaurant and wine cellar. Decor is pretty 1930s bistro style. Food is simple and there more to accompany and complement the wines: cheese and charcuterie is the norm. Bernard has opted to present his wines by taste rather than by region, with delicate reds separated from the heavier versions. Waiters are knowledgeable, but you pay for this level of expertise; bank on 200f for an alcoholic dinner.

Chez Louisette
(R)S   *136 av. Michelet, Marché Vernaison, 93 St Ouen, 40 12 21 98, no cc, open during the hours of the Marché aux Puces on Sat, Sun and Mon from 1-6 pm (Porte de St Ouen or Porte de Clignancourt)*

Straight out of a stage-set – the sort of place where you long to get every customer's face on film, but daren't for fear of a punch-up. Very rough and ready, very cheap and very cheerful (although the waitress won't go out of her way to hide a bad mood). This is the favourite local for stallholders from the nearby Marché aux Puces (flea market) hence the topics of conversation which tend to revolve around antiques, successful purchases, successful sales ... and the mug who paid all that money for those fake gold cufflinks! Don't get cross if the waitress ignores you – you're not paying for the service, nor really for the food, though the salt beef is recommended. Do as the locals do and avoid desserts which are plastic and tired. What you do pay for (approx 150f for a basic 3-course, ungastronomic tummy-filler) is the atmosphere and chatter.

Comtesse du Barry
(R)S   *23 av. de Wagram, 46 22 17 38 (Etoile)*

A chain of classy, gastronomic boutiques throughout the capital, this one being the best. The ideal place to sample all those food presents you intend taking home with you. Specialities originate from south-west France – foie gras (a number of varieties), pâtés, conserves and cassoulets. You can sample to your heart's content with wine served by the glass, carafe or bottle. Two courses go for 80f, three for 150f.

Paul et France
(R)ML   *27 av. Niel, 47 63 04 24, all cc, cl Sat lunch, Sun (Ternes)*

For years the Paul et France has been one of the arrondissement's respected tables. In 1992 chef-proprietor Georges Romano served his last meal at the restaurant. The new régime has received a modest welcome from the French press, which praised such dishes as turbot aux quinze épicés, agneau de Lozère aux ravioles de chèvre. The wine list, with a good selection at the 150f mark, has won a nod of approval, as has the lunch menu at 230f. Budget around 400f in the evenings. I look forward to revisiting the restaurant – and to any reports from readers.

➤ Epicure 108
(R)SM   *108 r. Cardinet, 47 63 50 91, MC V, cl Sat lunch, Sun (Courcelles)*

This unprepossessing street that stretches across the no-man's-land from the posh Etoile quarter to the bohemian of Montmartre is home, at least along this early stretch, to many cheap bar-restaurants and Alsatian restaurants. In amongst the refuelling stops offering lunch at 60f comes this gastronomic oasis. Take market-fresh ingredients, a textbook of classic French dishes and add a Japanese genius. Tetsu Goya's magic touch in the kitchen makes mealtimes an adventure; in his elegant modern dining room the low key decor belies the gastronomic fireworks. The neighbouring table was practically whimpering over a boudin blanc de poissons et grenouilles et lentilles vertes and I almost regretted following my impulse in ordering just a simple plate of vegetables – to save myself for the main course. I needn't have worried. A light and wonderful tower of thin slices of veg, suffused with a dill and tomato aromatic vinaigrette. Main courses were equally imaginative. Fried crisp ginger on a smoked salmon steak topped with crème fraîche, genius. Game, in season, is a speciality. Desserts brought croqignoles de chocolat à la marmelade de poires. This turned out to be little pastry parcels of chocolate that explode gently in the mouth with a pear purée. Four courses for just 170f and a wine list that is very haute de gamme, although a surprisingly low representation from Alsace considering the nature of the menu – still has a good average at 250f. Arrowed for the food.

Les Béatilles
(R)SM   *127 r. Cardinet, 42 27 95 64, V MC DC, cl Sat lunch, Sun, Aug (Courcelles)*

Understated decor, and a similarly discreet touch in the kitchen, makes this a good choice for quiet evenings à deux. An appreciative clientele comes from far and wide for the Beatilles' upmarket extension of the surf and turf concept – shrewd and successful marriages between seafood and meats. A croustillant of lard and salmon and the inspired mixture of scallops and pigs' trotters mark the restaurant out for originality. Lunch menu at 130f and evening selections at 180f and 230f do not include wine. Pay around 350f à la carte.

Les Terrasses
(R)S   *172 r. Cardinet, 42 26 74 44, AE V MC, cl weekends (Courcelles)*

On this particularly unattractive stretch of the Cardinet, opposite a noisy railway yard, is a pleasant little restaurant with a garden terrace at the rear. As well as the main menus at 76f and 126f there is a low calorie health-conscious alternative meal at 53f. The restaurant has a low-smoking policy, asking fumeurs to moderate their puffing.

Le Champart
(R)S   *132 r. Cardinet, 42 27 36 78, V MC, cl Sat lunch, Sun (Courcelles)*

A warm welcome at this cheerful auberge. If the waitress is busy when you arrive, the chef will wipe his hands on his apron and step out of the kitchen to show you to a table. Locals appreciate the sturdy food and smiling service and opt for such choices as the salad of chicken livers with raspberry vinaigrette, before the reliable filet mignon and good old-fashioned crème caramel. The set menu is 118f, wine from a tiny selection averages about 130f but a glass of the patron's choice is 28f. Budget 200f à la carte.

Graindorge
(R)SM   *15 r. de l'Arc de Triomphe, 47 54 00 28 (Etoile)*

After a long period of providing flat food in a flat atmosphere, the restaurant is born again – appropriately as a Belgian eatery. Under stylish 1930s lamps smoked eel pâté with leeks and Flanders stews are served, a refreshing change from the classic and nouvelle alternatives of the Champs Elysées.

18th ARRONDISSEMENT

(Paris 75018)

Montmartre dominates the 18th arrondissement. From the flash of Pigalle to the trash of the Clignancourt fleamarket, the silhouette of the Sacré Coeur gives an exotic edge to the skyline. The Basilica marks the centre of Paris' last remaining village.

Montmartre was always a village. Originally outside the city limits, it had the benefit of being outside the city's jurisdiction. So when the cancan was banned from the theatres of Paris, the bals publics of Montmartre welcomed clients to their dance floors, where the shameless gavotte was performed *sans dessous*, by the prostitutes of the hill.

Today a sanitised version of the dance is the finale of the floor show at the Moulin Rouge, named for the windmills that once dotted the hill. Renoir's quaint Moulin de la Galette can still be glimpsed here.

With so many glorious musical and artistic associations, it is no wonder that the hill is amongst France's most tourist-packed attractions. Yet despite the awful place du Tertre, with its permanent rush hour of tourists, artists, waiters and souvenir hustlers, the constant bleep-bleep of coaches reversing by the meringue domes of the basilica and the wall-to-wall oils and watercolours of a Paris so idealised they could make a postcard blush, Montmartre remains true to its past. Timeless and secluded private mansions lie behind locked gates, rickety steps climb pavements so steep that they have bannisters in the middle of the street. Relish the pig-out joy of frites under a 19th century lamp with the city spread at your feet, a midnight crêpe and modern jazz in the cramped basement of Le Tire-Bouchon, waiters dancing with their patronnes and caissières at 3 am.

The visitors climb the hill from the metro – or perhaps take the cable car up the final slopes. The Montmartrois loiter in the rue Lepic, with its twists, turns, markets and little food shops. The Europe-in-14-days crowd buys naïve pictures of empty squares and colourful churches. The wittier explorer discovers the outrageously surreal melting wristwatch at the gift shop of the Espace Dali, a Swiss-run museum devoted to the creations and sounds of the great artist – where the fantastically wealthy may even buy an exhibit or two.

Montmartre is the home of the tiny Parisian vineyard, an exclusive cemetery and more than one alleyway or face that might have been painted by Lautrec or the Bohemians of its glorious past.

Montmartre's past poverty is today's nostalgia. The 18th has its modern squalor as well – impoverished quarters, where today's less wealthy communities create their own distinct districts.

The lower slopes of Montmartre lead to the bustling crossroads of Barbés Rochechouart – home of Tati. Tati is the quarter's bargain basement, where security guards have to keep at bay the hordes of local shoppers determined to secure a pair of trousers at 10f, a skirt at 15f or an entire wardrobe for under 200f. The carnival spirit of the January sales tumbles all year round, and it is not just the locals who come here.

Since Kylie Minogue wore an outfit inspired by Tati's own-label pink gingham, and Hockney painted the pattern, the well-do-do habitués of the St Honoré have put on dark glasses and Hermès scarves to join in the scrum. There is even a story of a world leader who arrived late for a summit meeting, because the lure of the Tati racks proved too strong.

This is the heart of the Goutte d'Or district, where Arab and African shops lure visitors who ignore the graffiti to explore a true community quarter – an antidote to the sanitised chrome and glass wonderland of the city centre.

Of course fashionable Parisians have been coming north for years, hunting the bargains at the expansive fleamarket, the Marché aux Puces at Clignancourt. Don't expect to find a bargain, unless you've plans to shop before dawn, but should you find that glorious 18th century escritoire you've always wanted for the study, the good news is that there is no duty payable on antiques.

Marché bd. Ornano, Tue, Fri, Sun (Simplon); Crimée, bd. Ney, Wed, Sat (Porte de la Chapelle); Barbés, bd. de la Chapelle, Wed, Sat (Barbés Rochechouart); bd. Ney, Thu, Sun (Porte de Ste Ouen); r. Ordener, Wed, Sat (Guy Mocquet). All 7 am-1.30 pm. Covered Marché La Chapelle, r. de l'Olive (Marx Dormoy), Tue-Sat 8 am-1 pm, 3.30-7.30 pm, Sun 8 am-1 pm. Fleamarket (Porte de Clignancourt) Sat, Sun, Mon, 7 am-7.30 pm.

Festival de la Butte Montmartre, end of June.

HOTELS

Prima Lepic
(H)M 29   *r. Lepic, 46 06 44 64, V MC (Abbesses)*

If you were to imagine a typical Montmartre hotel, it would be the ever-popular Prima Lepic. At one of the twists in the winding rue Lepic street market that climbs the hill from the boulevard Clichy to Montmartre itself, the hotel is a narrow six-storey cluster of 40 rooms. Small and traditionally furnished, the simple bedrooms, with their stark old-fashioned bathrooms, are sought after by those who eschew marbling and heated towel rails in favour of traditional Parisian style. The place is under the eye, thumb and wing of Madame Reloug who scours the flea markets for bedside tables and chairs for the never-ending furnishing and refurbishment programme. Doubles cost around 350f per night and there are three 'family' apartments for 500-700f. Breakfast is served in the packed trompe l'oeil garden salon and luggage can be left in the lobby which is decorated as a Montmartre square. Off the lobby is a nicely fitted washroom, where late departing guests returning for their bags can have a final wash and brush up before catching the evening flight home.

Titania
(H)S   *70 bis bd. Ornano, 46 06 43 22, no cc (Porte de Clignancourt)*

Never mind the darned candlewick bedspreads, the cold floors on the moonlit pad to the bathroom, the low wattage bulbs; forget the shabby lift and the dimly-lit passages – this is the Paris hotel where impoverished writers should live out their days. The flea market is just a hundred yards away and it was outside the window that Paris' last great gangland shoot-out took place. This is a world away from the touristy Montmartre side of the 18th. Whenever film companies require an unfashionable unmodernised hotel for location filming, they call Mme Sautour and book a room. St Exupéry, author of *Le Petit Prince,* lived here for two years and I first discovered Paris at the age of 18 from these large and simply furnished rooms. Madame is the châtelaine of my memories and since the days, a decade since, when I graduated to more luxurious lodgings, I've missed her eccentric ways. She always keeps the reception salon in pristine condition. Antique furniture, a million vases and plastic covers on the seats. People should keep off the furniture; cats may, and do, wander freely, knocking over pots of plants in the courtyard and glaring at visitors in the window. I remember the dawn chorus of Madame shrieking admonition at the unfortunate chambermaids protesting their innocence in the matter of disappearing handtowels. I remember the wide smile of welcome and the slap when I left without hanging up my room key. When I returned about five years ago Madame was not there and I mourned a vanished era. But to my delight, the day I found myself in the Clignancourt flea market and popped back to the Titania for the Entrée's sake, there, with her hair and smile as firmly fixed as ever, Madame presided over the reception desk. A couple of weeks later I booked a room and found everything as before. Rooms are still only 130f for a double – around 200f with shower. No breakfast, but plenty of bakers and sandwich bars nearby.

Regyn's Montmartre
(H)M   *18 pl. des Abbesses, 42 54 45 21 (Abbesses or Pigalle)*

Place des Abbesses is a real live, fully functioning village square. It just so happens France's capital is down the hill. Church, trees, pigeons, benches where old men spend their days watching pretty girls go by. Like Hôtel Tim nearby the Hôtel Regyn has been included here more for its location than any outstanding character or architecture. Rooms 44, 46, 48, 54, 56 and 58 are the ones to ask for – all with outstanding views over the capital. No. 50 overlooks Sacré Coeur. The welcome also deserves a mention. The owner, Monsieur Cadin, is an active member of Montmartre life – guests here benefit from good bank rates he has negotiated and special attention in nearby restaurants. Rooms are simple, small and functional, priced more for their location than decor – from 400f for a double.

Hôtel Tim Montmartre
(H)M   *11 pl. Emile Goudeau, 42 55 74 79, A AE V (Abbesses)*

> A chain hotel (and it shows) but not many chains have views like this
> one. Only stay if you can get a room on the 4th and 5th floors for a
> stunning Parisian panorama. Otherwise you'll look out onto the pretty
> little place Emile Goudeau (whose trees are a bird sanctuary in
> summer – beware the dawn chorus). Rooms are functional, decor is
> pinks and blues. Views aside I'd recommend this one for its prices
> alone (400-450f isn't bad for a base within walking distance from the
> Moulin Rouge and Montmartre).

Hôtel Utrillo
(H)M   *7 r. Aristide Bruant, 42 58 13 44 (Abbesses or Blance)*

> A competitor to the Hôtel de l'Ermitage nearby for value and welcome.
> Well located between Montmartre (above) and Pigalle (far enough
> below). Monsieur and Madame Foudrain have been doing up the
> Utrillo bit by bit as budgets allow – rooms are extremely comfortable
> and well-equipped, perhaps lacking in imaginative decor. But at these
> prices – 400f for a double – it matters little. Breakfast is a generous 32f
> buffet served in the old cellars below (modernisation a bit overdone
> here).

L'Ermitage
(H)S   *24 r. Lamarck, 42 64 79 22 (Lamarck Caulaincourt)*

> More home than hotel thanks to the unfailing welcome of Monsieur
> and Madame Canipel who fell in love with this Napoleon III building
> 18 years ago. With just 11 rooms, this is a very personal hotel – clean,
> functional, unluxurious and not everyone's choice of decor. It matters
> little. The location (just 150m from the Sacré Coeur), the pretty garden
> and the welcome more than compensate. Rooms 11 and 12 have their
> own private terraces – good for summer breakfasts. Otherwise go for
> the 2nd floor rooms with garden views, and nos. 6 and 10 for views
> over Parisian rooftops. No. 8 is strictly for budgeters only. Prices are
> good for this touristy area – 400f including breakfast for a double, 280f
> for a single. Advance booking advised.

RESTAURANTS

Kokolion
(R)M   *62 r. d'Orsel, 42 58 24 41, MC V, cl Sun and Mon pm, open until 11.30 pm
(Abbesses)*

> Don't be put off by the strange orange railings outside and grim-
> looking door. Once inside this well-located restaurant in the heart of
> Montmartre, all is friendly, discreet, unpretentious. Cooking borders

on 'nouvelle' but the chef allows his own originality to seep into most dishes. Menus change regularly – bank on at least 250f for a three-courser. Clientele are theatre-goers, theatre critics, actors and the occasional tourist.

L'Homme Tranquille
(R)S   *81 r. de Martyrs, 42 54 56 28, no cc, cl Aug and Mon, open 7-11.30 pm (Pigalles or Abbesses)*

Many's the time I've left a Montmartre eatery with a big hole in my wallet as well as my stomach after an overpriced, ungastronomic tourist rip-off. L'Homme Tranquille is one of the few establishments in this tourist zone not to fall into this category. Good, cheap, honest and interesting. Ignore the shabby exterior and the unluxurious interior – high standards are reserved for the food. The Saint Marcellin, a rich soft cheese served hot, is a delectable must; likewise the rich mushroom pâté. The 100f menu changes regularly (always a good sign) but I wouldn't care if it didn't. Every dish sampled to date has been a winner. Wines also well priced starting at a little over 60f. Decor is fun, young, basic – like most of the clientele.

La Table de l'Oie
(R)S   *14 r. Ferdinand Flocon, 46 06 72 01, all cc, cl Sat lunch and Sun (Jules Joffrin)*

Unless you stray behind Montmartre your Paris tourist route is unlikely to lead you to what is surely one of the capital's best value eateries. Simple decor, friendly welcome. On Saturday nights tables are pushed together to make room for the jazz musicians. Cuisine is plentiful, rich and excellent value with a strong influence from south-west France – a curry of moules, duck breast served with peach, and wicked puds served with local table wines and perhaps an Armagnac to finish off. Bank on 150f for more than you can eat at dinner and a 65f lunch menu.

➤ Le Restaurant
(R)M   *32 r. Véran, 42 23 06 22, AE MC V, cl Sun and Mon lunch (Abbesses)*

It is the heady aroma of exotic spices that welcomes the visitor to the light and bright corner restaurant tucked away behind the better known streets of Lepic and Abbesses. And it is the witty and original flavourings and seasonings added to conventional ingredients that makes this cool and tranquil restaurant rather special. Clean walls, fashionably rough hewn, sport paintings and mirrors and an eclectic collection of screens and rambling plants divide the dining room into more intimate sections. The aromatic scent of the kitchen pervades everywhere, circulated by the breeze through the trellised windows. Unobtrusive modern furnishings do not detract from the calm and welcoming ambiance and single diners seem to be appreciated as much as couples and groups, not shunted into a corner for daring to read at table. The spices and scents continue through the handwritten menu. From the 148f lunch menu I selected an asparagus mousse with sweetcorn vinaigrette, light, smooth and piquant. Rascasse à l'étouffe de légumes de la bruille niçoise was a vegetable lover's dream, each texture matched with a cannily selected spice. Forsaking the spiced crème brulée I was seduced by as varied a selection of sorbets as ever I've tasted. From the sharpest of apricot to the smoothest of Charentais melon. The bill of fare changes regularly and on my last visit canard and cochon featured on the lunchtime and evening menu. A la carte comes to around 250f per head. But offers such mouthwatering temptations as bone marrow tart with wine, stewed onions and oyster omelettes, depending on the season. A relatively young but well-considered wine list complements the brief carte with a good selection at the 180f mark. Chef owner Yves Peladeau wins an arrow for originality and value.

Le Maquis
(R)S   *69 bd. Caulaincourt, 42 59 76 07, MC V (Lamarck Caulaincourt)*

Only a hint of pastel greens update the traditional beige and clay colours of a Montmartre café. And the neatness of the decor and staff suggest that this restaurant is out for a little more than the local clientele. The boulevard Caulaincourt is one of those Montmartre thoroughfares that are bisected by two-storey staircases masquerading as side streets. Residents, from mustachioed tradesmen to the dotty and bewigged concierge with trowelled make-up and Piaf-pencilled eyebrows, drop in for the 62f lunch menu, as do visitors foresaking the more touristic bistros of the quarter. Portions are hearty and the style is friendly – you feel that your plate has been loaded by a concerned grandmother suspicious that your evenings are frittered away with TV dinners. I try to nab a window table and choose à la carte. A feuilleté Roquefort was a little doughy, but savoury nonetheless on a cold day. The Thon à la Provençale was more than acceptable. A fair wine list. Expect to pay 200f.

Les Chants du Piano
(R)M   *10 r. Lambert, 42 62 02 14, all cc (Château Rouge)*

A charming dining room with a remarkably good value menu – lunch at 149f – has been a favourite of the quarter for some time. The imaginative cuisine owed much to the inspiration of its creator Michel Derbane, now decamped to Les Halles (see Le Petit Bourbon 1st arrondissement). Recent reports welcomed.

Marie Louise
(R)M   *15 r. Championnet, 46 06 86 55, V MC DC, cl Sun, Mon, Aug (Porte Clignancourt)*

The section of the rue Championnet to the east of the boulevard Ornano is where the locals of the 18th choose to eat. Here amongst the sweat shops and laundries of this generally poor quarter is a united nations of cuisine – West Indian, Vietnamese, even Portuguese traditions. Not to mention the cous cous and pizzas served in the bars. For French food at its most familiale drop by chez Marie Louise, Jean Coillot's traditional little formica, copper and lamp-shade-style dining room. Loyal customers who've moved away from the poor streets of the 18th still come back for more. Old-fashioned veal dishes you'd have found on any Paris corner forty years ago fill the menu. Tête de veau, rognons in Madeira and côte de veau grand-mère. But nostalgia keeps just this side of the price column. You should pay 200-250f per head including wine.

La Crémaillère 1900
(R)SM   *15 pl. du Tertre, 46 06 58 59, all cc (Anvers then funicular)*

On the most tourist-packed square in all France, where artists peddle views of the Moulin Rouge, silhouettes and caricatures, there is no shortage of tables. The Crémaillère offers the best choice of simple food – a good onion soup, big salads and fair grills. Inside the nursery circus decor is suitably retro. Garden tables are set in the kitschest of imitation village squares – there's even a windmill. It is a little like dining in a postcard. Menus begin at 110f for lunch. Including wine à la carte comes to around 300f.

Charlot 1er
(R)M   *128 bis bd. de Clichy, 45 22 47 08, all cc (Clichy)*

Not to be confused with the neighbouring Charlot Roi des Coquillages (9th arrondissement) this is a standard seafood brasserie. Pay around 300f.

19th ARRONDISSEMENT

(Paris 75019)

Don't, please don't, ignore the unassuming 19th. A great sweep of périphérique and railway track might leave you under the impression that there's little to bother with between the ring road and the boulevard de la Villette. But ...

But indeed, who needs the Seine? The canals that once transported coal through France and water to the capital's fountains, still flow through the newly created quarter of La Villette; strolls at the waterside are a way of life here.

Once the stinking abattoir district, the modern Cité des Sciences, with its exhibitions, concert hall, gardens, planetarium and globe-shaped cinema screen is the Epcot that EuroDisney forgot.

Me, I prefer the open air: sitting by the canal, leaning over the bridges at the locks, just whiling away an afternoon on the quaysides, each one named after a great river region of France – the Loire, Seine, Charente, Gironde; a coffee in a local bar, where the meat workers – yes, the slaughter business has not quite disappeared – wipe bloody hands on grubby work clothes and read the sporting papers, prove that La Villette is not yet the Technokid Yuppidrome that was planned.

And, most wonderful of all, I can escape into the deep French countryside, without stepping across the parish boundaries. I will be crossing dramatic gorges, and climbing mountains. For here is the Parc des Buttes Chaumont. From the outside the park is a modest-sized garden with traffic all around. But within, it is a vast region in its own right – dramatic rocky cliffs, waterside strolls, woodland paths and a complete escape from the city. Originally a quarry, the remaining hills and basin were a putrid mass of muck and trash. Then Haussmann created what to my mind was his St Paul's, a multi-tiered park using the natural environment and outrageous artifice, flooding the quarries into a winding lake, then raising the bald hills even higher, piling rocky peaks to be crossed by suspension bridges and crowned with a temple of love. If you seek a memorial, no need to visit the grave at Père Lachaise (see 20th) – just look around you.

It takes hours to take in the entire park at leisure and while it may not have the vast expanses of the Bois de Boulogne it can still boast at least one excellent restaurant. On Sunday mornings the park is the rendez-vous for the jogging club whose members negotiate rocks and spaniels with enviable skill as they bound around the mounds.

Marché ave. Jean Jaurés, Tue, Thu, Sun (Ourq); r. Joinville, Thu, Sun (Crimée); pl. des Fêtes, Tue, Fri, Sun (pl. des Fêtes); av. Porte Brunet, Wed, Sat (Danube); bd. de la Villette, Wed, Sat (Colonel Fabien). All 7 am-1.30 pm. Covered markets: r. Riquet (Riquet) and av. Sécrétan (Bolivar), both Tue-Sat 8 am-1 pm, 4-7.30 pm, Sun 8 am-1 pm.

Festivals: Halle that Jazz, July, jazz festival at La Villette. Cinéma en plein air, July-August.

HOTELS

Hôtel du Parc des Buttes Chaumont
(H)SM   *1 pl. Armand Carrel, 42 08 08 37, V MC DC (Laumière)*

A room at less than 300f with a clean and tiled bathroom is very much the traditional Parisian bargain. With a slightly better than average breakfast. Don't come here for the decor but for the view. Demand a room on one of the top floors facing the park. My room looked over the enchanting lake and gorge of the hilly wonderland (see above), a magical oasis in the heart of such a residential quarter. Polite staff will book local fringe theatres for you – there is a good music-hall tradition of rough and ready song-shows. Occasionally open air theatre in the parks can brighten even a November evening. Be prepared to suffer the toots and hoots of Parisian traffic sounds into the night. There are smarter business class hotels a few hundred yards away around La Villette but Entrée readers are made of sterner stuff than to opt out of the quarter's own identity!

Laumière
(H)S   *4 r. Petit, 42 06 10 77, MC V (Laumière)*

This is the only hotel of the quarter to make it into the Michelin and doubtless the French inspectors felt, as I did, that after traipsing round the district it was best of a mediocre bunch. A very helpful and cheery reception staff provide a warm welcome in the modern and bright 1st floor reception. Rooms however, though clean and soundproofed, are ill lit with tired-looking bedspreads and towels. Good value at under 300f for a double room.

RESTAURANTS

➤Rendez-vous de la Marine
(R)S   *14 q. de la Loire, 42 49 33 40, cl Sun, Mon (Jaurès)*

On the banks of the canal basin is one of the least pretentious pleasures in all Paris. This is a real bistro du port and to my mind the best reason in the world for visiting the 19th. The young whizz-kids of the Cité-des-Sciences have the designer brasseries that skirt La Villette, the expense account conférenciers have the Cochon d'Or and the Pavillon Puebla (see below), but the real people of the 19th have the Rendez-vous. You will have to book because every table is always taken. Although (or perhaps because) the place is always packed, there is always a convivial and hearty welcome from the host. No matter how busy the staff always have time to be friendly to regulars. And those regulars are families with their children, retired couples arguing past disputes, lovers and workers. As many tables as possible are squeezed into a room whose walls are covered with pictures of the famous from JFK to BB, via Liz and Yul. The kitchen is no less warm-hearted. Of the school that believes that the white of a plate should never be uncovered, its portions are enormous. A starter salad is bigger than a main course anywhere else. Rare meats melt into hearty sauces, salt cod is flaky and chewy, haricot beans and other vegetables are market fresh. The style of food ranges from Normandy specialities to the house favourite paella (24 hours notice required).

For dessert, apple tart flambéed in Calvados looked tempting but I succumbed to the gigantic profiteroles topped with home-made chocolate. For a two course meal you can pay under 100f, for three courses à la carte 150f should suffice – but three courses require a healthy appetite. There is a simple but sensibly priced wine selection. Arrowed for a familiale atmosphere, good old-fashioned food and a genuinely happy welcome, all in a charming location.

➤ Pavillon Puebla
(R)ML   *parc des Buttes Chaumont, 42 08 92 62, MC V, cl Sun, Mon, Aug (Buttes Chaumont)*

The park (see above) is one of Paris' hidden delights. It is unbelievable that you could lose yourself in the country in such a small urban garden – but you could spend more than half an hour over hill and dale, unless you ask someone to point you to the right path for the Pavillon Puebla. Not facing the breathtaking view of the temple but tucked away at the foot of another hill is this one-time hunting lodge. An autumnal retreat or a summer terrace the restaurant is very much a year-round venue. When we invited Parisian friends from the fashionable west of the city to dine in this downmarket suburb they consented politely – can there be a decent restaurant in such a quarter was the unspoken reaction. The answer is an unequivocal Yes. Christian Vergès' Pavillon has the twin merits of being one of the city's gastronomic high spots and a superbly run restaurant. As elegant as her surroundings Madame supervises the service of her husband's imaginative creations. The cuisine is of the south-west and sauces are something of a house speciality. From the autumn fruit accompaniment to the quenelles of warm rabbit pâté, through the vinaigrette with the roquefort to the triumphant finale, a soup of marinated fruits and sorbet. Steaks are prepared just so and a niçoise of fish is delicately perfumed with basil. A wisely compiled wine list complements the meal. A la carte could cost 500f but the menu of the day provides a set five-course lunch for just 230f. The arrow would be deserved for the location alone but for quality and the value of the menu it is awarded to an all-round treasure.

Le Pavillon du lac
(R ST)M   *parc des Buttes Chaumont, 42 02 08 97, MC V (Buttes Chaumont)*

The other side of the park to the Puebla (above) this has the benefit of a view across the remarkable lakes to the hilltop lookout. The mealtime menu is expensive and not in the class of the Puebla but during the day the restaurant is a good old-fashioned salon de thé. Old ladies muffled in moth-eaten furs squint myopically at the dog walkers and honeymoon meanderers taking the hidden footpaths to the Temple of Love. Families enjoy the promised ice-cream and at around 35f for a glace, it won't break the bank.

→**Au Cochon d'Or**
(R)ML   *192 av. Jean-Jaurès, 42 45 46 46, all cc (Porte de Pantin)*

> Beef and pork are on the menu and near perfect steaks have kept this restaurant packed practically every night these past seventy years. Of course when the Ayral family first started grilling, pan-frying and casseroling the clientele did not arrive in limousines. It is only in recent years that the Cochon d'Or and its neighbours along this stretch of the avenue Jean-Jaurès have employed a line of peaked-capped commissionaires to assist guests to and from their cars. For at the beginning of the century this was the quarter of the abattoirs and the butchers – who knew their meat – would not have settled for a cheese sandwich and green salad. Just as Les Halles encouraged some legendary tables in its market days the meat markets nurtured the Cochon d'Or. Today, with the business and executive trade at La Villette, the welcome is smarter but the quality remains the same, with my Parisian friends declaring this the home of the finest filet mignon and the best tête de veau in the east of the city. Grands crus abound in the cellar and this is the sort of meal that demands a splashing out on wine budgets, so expect to pay around 500f for a full meal à la carte. If you are counting the cost a fair menu at 240f will not disappoint.

Dagorno
(R)M   *192 av. Jean-Jaurès, 40 40 09 39, MC V AE (Porte de Pantin)*

> It may have a commissionaire on the pavement, but the restaurant is not in the same league as the Cochon d'Or next door. But it passes itself off pretty creditably, so long as you avoid comparing the meat dishes. A marbre de lotte et homard is amongst the choices on a reasonably priced 168f 'vin-compris' set menu – although à la carte would set you back double the price. Open until after midnight, which makes it a popular choice for the trendy types heading to, or from, the Zenith rock venue.

Le Sancerre
(R)M   *13 av. Corentin Cariou, 40 36 80 44, all cc, cl Sat, Sun, Aug (Corentin Cariou)*

> Another of the slaughterhouse eateries – today's business clientele is drawn from La Villette opposite. Amongst countless traditional, kosher and halal butchers, it is not surprising that the house specialises in meat dishes, although the daily specials usually include a decent alternative. A la carte lunches work out at around 300f, but there is a menu at 110f. Good portions, simply but well cooked, and standard desserts such as a wedge of tarte tatin swimming in Calvados and flambéed to inspire the national grid. An excellent wine list includes the house Sancerre served liberally and charged as per the amount supped.

20th ARRONDISSEMENT

(Paris 75020)

Between the 19th and the 12th, from the farthest reach of La République to the ring road, the last arrondissement of Paris is famous for its residents, more than a million of whom receive visitors every day.

Alas, they can no longer speak to us, but their words have already spoken volumes.

For they are the residents of the greatest necropolis in the city, Père Lachaise cemetery. The roll of honour is seemingly endless: Oscar Wilde, Sarah Bernhardt, Marcel Proust, Molière, Colette and Rossini. Their followers pass through the various entrances of this surprisingly welcoming and attractive city of the departed.

Lovers come to the grave of Abelard and Héloïse; refugees and ex-patriots bring flowers to the cenotaphs of the nations; rock fans carry guitars and their own music to the graffiti-covered memorial to Jim Morrison.

Political pilgrims lay tributes at the Mur des Fédérés cemetery wall, against which were massacred the final 147 martyrs of the Paris Commune, shot with the final bullets of 1871.

People visit for the peace and calm. They come for the dramatic masonry and the wry epitaphs, to smile at Alice B. Toklas's name written so small behind the shared headstone that boldly proclaims the name of Gertrude Stein. Sometimes they come for funerals. It seemed as though half of Paris paid its final respects to the great Yves Montand who died recently. Now he lies in the memorial grounds that protect the legendary first lady of the quarter – Paris' little sparrow, Edith Piaf herself.

Piaf is remembered in the surrounding streets, cafés and homes of Belleville and Ménilmontant. The streets and people of whom she sang can still be seen in the quarter.

A plaque marks her birthplace at no. 12 rue de Belleville. At no. 5 rue Crespin-du-Gast (a few feet across the border in the 11th) her friends dedicate a museum to her life and music. Bernard Marchois is happy to show visitors around, Monday to Thursday (telephone first on 43 55 52 72) – and a donation to the museum funds is always welcome. Often one meets up with musicians and composers who worked with la môme Piaf, and can hear stories of a Paris that is, alas, disappearing fast.

Marché r. Belgrand, Wed, Sat (Gambetta); bd. Davout, Tue, Fri (Porte de Montreuil); bd. Mortier, Thu, Sun (St Fargeau); r. des Pyrénées, Thu, Sun (Gambetta); pl. de la Réunion, Thu, Sun (Alexandre Dumas); r. du Télégraphe, Wed, Sat (Télégraphe). All 7 am-1.30 pm.
Fleamarket, av. de la Porte de Montreuil, Sat, Sun, Mon (Porte de Montreuil).

HOTELS

Pyrénées Gambetta
(H)S   *12 av. Père Lachaise, 47 97 76 57, MC V AE (Gambetta)*

Finding a hotel in the 20th is not as easy as it might sound. There is the usual selection of anonymous sales-rep accommodation and a smattering of the most basic one- and two-star stop-overs. Still, around the place Gambetta, at the northern side of Père Lachaise, one or two Entrée candidates announce themselves. The Pyrénées Gambetta is just around the corner from the Théâtre National de la Colline – worth a visit for theatre buffs – and at the gateway to the northern necropolis. A warm and cheerful welcome from both day and night staff is encouraging and around 300f pays for a respectable room. Wardrobes make a grand canopy over the bed in the top price rooms and all are fitted well for a two-star at this price range. Soundproofed windows guaranteed a quiet night's sleep. Bathrooms are basic, but attractive and clean. There is a taxi rank outside the front door for cabs to the airport.

Palma
(H)SM   *77 av. Gambetta, 46 36 13 65, all cc (Gambetta)*

You won't be inspired to redecorate the spare room at home after a night at the modernised but bland Palma. Courteous and efficient staff, hair-dryers in the bathroom of a two-star hotel and convenient garage parking opposite. Pay around 350f a room, with compact bath to bring you ever closer to your knees.

Lilas Gambetta
(H)SM   *223 av. Gambetta, 43 62 85 60, MC V (Porte des Lilas)*

Modernised, soundproofed and comfortable rooms with hair-dryer and mini-bar for 360f with bath. Breakfast served in attractive little salon.

RESTAURANTS

La Fontaine aux Roses
(R)S   *27 av. Gambetta, 46 36 74 75, MC V, cl Sun lunch, Mon (Gambetta)*

As my father said: This is the sort of place you imagine when you talk about having a bite to eat in France – all the tables are packed, everyone is talking and everybody is enjoying the food. Unpretentious and relentlessly floral, this modest corner restaurant opposite Père Lachaise offers a good choice of reliable fare – traditional steaks, fricassée of quail, an imaginative range of fish dishes – on a set menu. Lunch is 103f, but dinner at 156f is excellent value, including a kir royale, bottle of house wine and coffee. No hidden extras. Appetising appetizers, a creditable feuilleté of asparagus and some rich and warming baked smoked salmon crêpes in generous portions. Ignore the bland brie and choose one of the homely desserts, nice fruit tart or enormous profiteroles. Cheery service and a good mix of genuinely local customers.

Aux Becs Finx
(R)M   44 bd. de Ménilmontant, 47 97 51 52, V MC AE, cl Sun, open until 9.30 pm (Père Lachaise)

A rather twee little trellised terrace outside this best known of the Père Lachaise eateries. The staff are as old as the decor and the food of their era is the most reliable. So opt for tête de veau and the bavette bordelaise rather than some of the more adventurous salmon creations. The cosy, ground floor dining room with its copper pots and spiral staircase is the perfect venue for a long drawn out gossip over a steaming casserole. Menus are 180 and 240f. A la carte around 350f.

Chantefable
(R ST)SM   93 av. Gambetta, 46 36 81 76, V MC DC, cl Sun hols (Gambetta)

Serendipity! We had walked for an hour and only found a pretty uninspiring dinner trough when, stomachs still rumbling, we came across this shining oasis. The lights, windows, mirrors and glasses positively twinkle their welcome across the road. And inside the friendly staff are no less cheery. On that first visit we just wanted a dessert to combat the dreary meal up the hill. No problem. Guided to a table under the terracotta ceiling of the bright and boldly floral front salon (more convivial than the quieter back section) we were treated with the same care that met diners taking the full dinner. Food is not disappointing. Reliable and good value for money. Escargots are generously served and a millefeuille of munster a savoury alternative. Noisettes of trout in herb mayonnaise delicious. Leave room for the scrummy desserts: a parfait of melting butterscotch was as light as a cloud and my pear sorbet in poire William liqueur as fluffy as could be. Budget 200f à la carte, or opt for the 89f menu, three courses and wine included.

Bistrot du XXe
(R)SM   44 r. du Sermelin, 48 97 20 30, all cc, cl Sat, Sun (St Fourgeau)

Do not stray from stews or you may well be disappointed. Fortunately the 86f and 120f menus are of the cassoulet variety, so that nourishing and warming dinners may be relied upon. The more adventurous aspects of the menu are as inconsistent as the decor – which ranges from rustic beams to mirror mosaic, via taverna plaster, exquisite tiled ceiling and formica. Service is friendly and the chef himself takes your order unless the kitchen is overworked. Our starters, a poêlon of cèpes and chaud froid of salmon and avocado were unimaginative and I drew the short straw when I chose a fish dish. A workmanlike butter sauce with capers failed to mask a very bland cod. Adequate cheeseboard, left on the table – a nice touch – is to be advised over the somewhat lumpen desserts. A fair wine list had a well-chosen range of burgundies at around 300f and beaujolais crus from 100f. Many half bottles.

La Chaumine
(R)S   *49 r. de la Chine, 43 66 73 25, MC V, cl Sun (Gambetta)*

Cheap and cheerful food from the Limousin prepared on the stone and served in a noisy dining room was never designed for the tourist trade. Duck standards and pâté munched in front of the television is not haute cuisine – but for an undemanding night off from serious gastronomy, this is how the locals enjoy themselves. Menus at under 50f and at 95f to suit the budget-conscious.

The Notaire on the Corner

The last Zinc bars of Paris

Paris, like many another city, has plenty of bars, a plethora of cafés and no shortage of brasseries, bistros and salons de thé. But it also has its Zincs – and they have a charm uniquely Parisian. A disappearing charm, but something special, nonetheless.

The Zincs are named after the polished metal bar tops seen in the photographs of Robert Doisneau and the Parisian films of the 1940s. It was in the 1820s when a provincial cabinet-maker, Emile Verrière, remembered the tin mines of his native Auvergne, that the shiny tin counters began to appear in the capital.

The Auvergnat patrons who ran the bars of Pigalle, the Bastille and Les Halles commissioned custom-made metallic counters for their establishments, and the clink of bottles and glass on zinc became as much a traditional sound of Paris as the accordion itself.

The Zincs were the birthplace of that most Parisian of music, the accordéon Java. The swinging rhythm of the Java was made famous by such street songstresses as Fréhel, the inspiration of Edith Piaf. The Java was so called after the rich southern accents of the barmen who called out 'Ca va?' in greeting to their customers at the Zincs.

An entire argot of bistro slang was born in the Zincs. Rough and ready Parisian *patois*, a little like East End cockney slang, was developed and grew across the metal counters. A glass of wine is a 'coup de jus'; one does not drink, one sprays ('On s'arrose') the corridor; an empty bottle is darkly referred to as a 'cadavre' (corpse); and a trip to the Zinc is euphemistically referred to as a visit 'chez le notaire du coin' – to the solicitor at the corner! The Zingeurs, who drink at the counter, kept the slang going over the years. After the war a glass of red wine became a 'Staline'.

A dictionary of the bistro slang, l'*Argot du Bistrot* by Robert Girault, is published by Editions Marval.

The atmosphere of the Zinc still permeates the busy executive chat and yuppy posing of today's Paris. Get the patron chatting about his zinc counter, and the locals will put down their glasses and start to tell their stories.

Some café-bars listed in the main section of this Entrée still retain the old zinc counters. I've included them in this selection of a dozen of Paris' few surviving Zincs:

1st arr - **Aux Deux Saules**
91 r. *St Denis, 42 36 46 57 (Les Halles)*

Despite the tacky plastic chairs outside, within this old shop is a true zinc counter, and wonderful tiled walls. Open every day.

Au Petit Ramoneur
74 r. *St Denis, 42 36 39 24 (Strasbourg-St Denis)*

Fifties style bar in this no-nonsense end of the rue St Denis, closed at weekends. 61f basic menu.

Le Rubis
10 r. *du Marché St Honoré, 42 61 03 34 (Pyramides)*

Something traditional in the up-and-coming restaurant quarter of the Rivoli-St Honoré district.

2nd arr - **Le Brin de Zinc ... et Madam**
50 r. *Montorgueil, 42 21 10 80 (Les Halles)*

A turn-of-the-century-style bar.

Le Brissemoret
5 r. *St Marc, 42 36 91 72 (rue Montmartre)*

Some of the original tin fittings to this traditional Zinc lure the experts. Traditional cuisine pleases the locals. Closed at weekends.

4th arr - **Le Petit Fer à Cheval**
30 r. *Vieille-du-Temple, 42 72 47 47 (St Paul)*

This tiny room can just about contain the huge sweep of the horseshoe bar, so chairs line the narrow pavement outside. Marais residents cycle over from all around the quarter to one of the last old style Zincs of the area.

5th arr - **Perraudin**
157 r. *St Jacques, 46 33 15 75 (St Michel)*

Ever-popular with students, not least due to the 59f lunch menu. Closed Saturday lunchtimes and Sundays.

6th arr - **Le Petit Zinc**
11 r. *St Benoît, 46 33 51 66 (St Germain-des-Près)*

Spend around 200f on a meal, in lively company. Open until
2 am.

7th arr - **Au Pied de Fouet**
45 r. *de Babylone, 47 05 12 27 (Sèvres-Babylone)*

Eccentric decor, from cartwheels to teapots, serves bistro
meals until early evening. Pay around 80f. Closed at
weekends.

11th arr - **Chardenoux**
1 r. *Jules Vallés, 43 71 49 52 (Charonne)*

A real piano sweep of a counter with genuine bistro
specialities served midweek. Spend around 200f on food.

Clown Bar
114 r. *Amelot, 43 55 87 35 (Filles-du-Calvaire)*

An appropriate name for the local bar of the Cirque d'Hiver
indoor circus. Lovely old posters and friezes, reliable food for
100-150f. Closed Sundays.

12th arr - **Le Square Trousseau**
1 r. *Antoine Vollon, 43 43 06 00 (Lédru-Rollin)*

A sweeping counter, on which are served meals costing
between 100-200f. Closed Sundays and Mondays.

English Spoken Here

English or, to be more accurate, American, is spoken everywhere that prices are tailored to the tourist trade. Paris has long been in love with the American dream – witness the scores of images of James Dean and Marilyn Monroe in every souvenir shop, boutique and diner – and Americans have always been far more effusive in their affections than their reserved English cousins when it comes to loving Paris.

So, wherever English is spoken the bill is the check, the town centre is downtown and the pavement is a sidewalk, no matter what your Collins dictionary says about 'l'addition, centre-ville and le trottoir'.

The international nature of Parisian life means that, however limited your French, you will be understood in most places. But do try to speak French. The Parisians really appreciate the effort – even if you only grunt, shrug your shoulders, gesticulate and utter a noun in an interrogative manner. Toilets, Meat, Box Office, Eiffel Tower are all words that, with the correct body language, can produce the same results as a Berlitz-graduated paragraph.

English is spoken wherever you see staff wearing a lapel badge showing a smiling face atop a Union Jack bow-tie, with the word 'welcome' printed to one side. The badges were introduced in 1992 by the Ministry of Tourism, and distributed to shops, airports, hotels and restaurants.

English and American restaurants – and pubs – abound. Other guides are filled with their addresses. If you really are homesick for fish and chips or a stateside snack, then stroll through Les Halles; you'll find plenty of opportunities to practise your English.

For information about the city use the 'phone. Dial 47 20 88 98 for entertainment news, or the American Express help line on (freephone) 05 20 12 02, which answers any questions you might have.

Banks British banks have branches throughout Paris. The main addresses are as follows:

Barclays
33 r. 4 September, 75002. 42 66 65 31 (Opéra)

Lloyds
43 bd. des Capucines, 75002. 42 61 51 25 (Opéra)
Midland
6 r. Piccini, 75016. 45 02 80 80 (Porte Maillot)

National Westminster
18 pl. Vendôme, 75001. 42 60 37 40 (Opéra)

American Express
Has its principal branch near the Opéra, 11 r. Scribe, 75009. 42 66 09 99.

British Eurocheque cards are accepted in many central branches of French banks, and their cash machines.

Book-shops

Spoilt for choice, when it comes to English language bookshops, the visitor to Paris has the best of British and American publishing to choose from. I spent one summer changing trains in Paris as I criss-crossed the country. My suitcase at the end creaked under the weight of the paperbacks I picked up en route.

Bretano's
37 av. de l'Opéra, 75002. 42 61 52 50. 10 am-7 pm, Mon-Sat. MC V (Opéra)

Good selection of English and French editions. A selection of discount bargains by the till that beat the price in the US and UK.

Calignani
224 r. de Rivoli, 75001. 42 60 76 07. 10 am-7 pm, Mon-Sat. MC V (Tuileries)

The first English bookshop on the continent retains an impressive selection of English language titles at the rear of the shop. Very old-fashioned in style, it is one of those establishments where customers and staff still converse in hushed whispers.

Shakespeare & Co
37 r. de la Bucherie, 75005. Open noon-midnight every day. No cc (Maubert Mutualité)

See section on the 5th arrondissement for more on this wonderful, eccentric bookshop selling new and second-hand editions, and still dispensing wisdom and sympathy as liberally as in the days of its founder, Sylvia Beach, Hemingway's mentor.

W H Smith
248 r. de Rivoli, 75001. 42 60 37 97. Open 9.30 am-7 pm. MC V (Concorde)

In the shadow of the Tuileries is a corner of some foreign field that is forever Victoria Station. A packed branch of Smiths, with a better selection of books than many of its UK sisters. Those who remember its first floor tea-room where Earl Grey and Agatha Christie welcomed ex-pats, will be sad to hear that it is no more. The space is filled with even more wonderful books.

Broad-casting BBC World Service radio can be heard in 648 khz, and Radio Four may occasionally be found on 198 khz (by avid Archers fans). Most hotels in the M and L categories will have satellite or cable TV.
   Satellite usually means Sky News, but cable brings BBC World Service Europe, with news and programmes from the UK. CNN is available on both Satellite and Cable. CBS Evening News is broadcast on France's Canal Plus (channel four) at 7.30 am weekdays. Essential viewing at around 9 am on France 3 is Alex Taylor's superb Continentales, a round-up of that day's news broadcasts from Britain and the rest of Europe. He also presents a midnight review of the papers.

Churches English language church services are held throughout the city:

Anglican
American Church, 65 q. d'Orsay, 75007 (Alma Marceau)
Church of Holy Trinity, 23 av. George V, 75008 (Alma Marceau)
Church of England, 5 r. d'Aguesseau, 75008 (Madeleine)
St George's English Church, 7 r. A-Vacquérie, 75016 (Kléber)

Methodist
Wesleyan Methodist, 4 r. Roquepine, 75008 (St Augustin)

Church of Scotland
17 r. Bayard, 75008 (F D Roosevelt)

Roman Catholic
St Joseph's Church, 50 ave Hoche, 75008 (Louis-Blanc)

Cinema   Paris has more cinemas than any other capital city – with a
choice of some 300 films every week. Details of movies and
showings can be found in newspapers, as well as the listings
magazines, *l'Officiel des Spectacles* (2f) and *Pariscope* (3f).
With first-run movies (often shown here months in advance of
the British première) the screens in the central areas
(especially the Les Halles and Champs Elysées cinemas)
usually show the original English language versions, subtitled
in French. Outside arrondissements feature dubbed showings.
In film listings the code v.o. means original language, v.f.
refers to the French version. There are scores of cinemas
showing classic movies of the past. Arty Warhol and Jarman
films play at the Ciné Beaubourg, next to the Pompidou
Centre, from mid-morning to midnight. Hollywood heyday
pictures are screened on the left bank, especially at the Action
cinemas. Hepburn, Garland, Monroe and Astaire are always to
be seen on the big screen. The videothèque and
cinemathèques also show English language films.

**Con-   The Consulate, rather than the Embassy, deals with most
sulates   tourist problems, from lost passports to legal difficulties.**

United Kingdom
16 r. d'Anjou, 75008, 42 66 91 42 (Concorde)

Eire
12 av. Foch, 75016, 45 00 20 87 (Etoile)

United States
2 r. St Florentin, 75001, 42 96 12 02 (Concorde)

Canada
35 av. Montaigne, 75008, 47 23 01 01 (F D Roosevelt)

Australia
4 r. Jean Rey, 75015, 40 59 33 00 (Bir Hakeim)

New Zealand
7 r. Léonard de Vinci, 75016, 45 00 24 11 (Victor Hugo)

Medical   For help and advice from English speaking staff:

The American Hospital in Paris
63 bd. Victor Hugo, 92202 Neuilly, 46 41 25 25 (Porte Maillot)
British American Pharmacy
1 r. Auber, 75009, 47 42 49 40, Mon-Sat, 8.30 am-8 pm (Opéra)

**News-
papers &
Magazines**   British newspapers arrive morning-fresh at most kiosks in the central Paris area. Most magazines can be found at W H Smith (see BOOKSHOPS). *Boulevard* is the title of the English language glossy magazine on Paris that might be found in an hotel bedroom. The *International Herald Tribune*, published in Paris, gives an American slant on the news, otherwise US Sunday papers can be bought, at great expense and several days later, from FNAC record stores. *France-USA Contacts* is a free magazine with useful English language small-ads, available at English-speaking venues listed on these pages, and trendy central restaurants and bars, as is *The Parisite*, an audaciously satirical newspaper, whose every outrageous story is 'a tissue of lies'. Witty, shocking, rude and well worth reading.

Shopping   English language shopping assistance is on hand at the big department stores:

Galeries Lafayette
40 bd. Haussmann, 75009, 42 82 36 40, Mon-Sat, 9.30 am-6.30 pm, all cc (Auber)

Printemps
64 bd. Haussmann, 75009, 42 82 50 00, Mon-Sat, 10 am-7 pm, all cc (Auber)

Samaritaine
19 r. de la Monnaie, 75001, 40 10 20 20, Mon-Sat, 9.30 am-7 pm, all cc (Pont Neuf)

Theatre   Paris has more plays running in any one week than the West End and Broadway combined. Many plays by British or American playwrights will be performed in the original tongue. Usually four or five British language productions are staged at any one time. The Théâtre Marie Stuart is home to more than one anglophone or bilingual company. Full theatre listings are available in the weekly guides (see under CINEMA). American musicals often feature in the repertoire of the Théâtre du Châtelet, and versions of popular British and American shows usually run at the Théâtre Mogador and the Casino de Paris. The floor shows at the Lido and Moulin Rouge are pretty bilingual.

Travelling from the Airport

Train   Shuttle buses from the terminals link to the RER station for
Line B joining the Metro system at Gare du Nord, Châtelet and
St Michel. Departures every 15 minutes. Journey time 25
minutes. Fare 33f.

Buses   Air France Shuttle from the terminals to Porte Maillot and the
Arc du Triomphe. Every 15 minutes. Journey time 35 minutes.
Fare 48f.
   Route 350 to Gare du Nord, Gare de L'Est. Every 20 minutes.
   Route 351 to Nation. Every 30 minutes. Departs from all
terminals. Cost 33f or 5 Metro tickets.
   New Roissybus Service to Opéra. Every 15 minutes from all
terminals. Fare 30f.

Taxis   Pay between 200-300f and allow 25-45 minutes.

Wine Hints from Jancis Robinson and
on Spirits from John Doxat

HOW TO READ A WINE LIST

Wine lists in France, just like their counterparts in British restaurants, can be confusing – and sometimes even terrifying, with the only affordable bottles hidden below a stack of great names at even greater prices. There are certain ground rules in their layout, however.

The most basic of wines made in France are called *vins de table*, and may well be listed under this heading, to differentiate them from wines with some sort of geographical designation, either *Appellation Contrôlée* (AC) or, slightly more lowly, *Vins de Qualité Supérieur* (VDQS). The 'house wine' in many French restaurants is of the simpler *vin de table* sort and may be described as Vin de la Maison, or Vin du Patron meaning 'our wine'. There are many branded table wines too, the sort that carry a brand name, and these should be listed under a special heading, *Vins de Marque*. There is also a newish breed of rather superior *vin de table* which is worth looking out for, and which may be listed under the heading *Vins de Table*, or the region where it was made, or under the general heading *Vins de Pays*. These are superior quality *vins de table* which are good enough to tag their provenance onto their name.

All other wines will usually be grouped under the heading of the region where they were made and, usually, split according to red wines (rouges) and whites (blancs). The following are the main wine regions of France, in the order in which they *usually* appear on a smart wine list (though there is, exasperatingly, no standard convention):

Champagne

Almost all champagne is dry, white and sparkling, and only the wines of the Champagne region in northern France may call their wines champagne. Other sparkling wines are Vins Mousseux, though they may boast on their label that they were made by the rigorous *méthode champenoise*.

Bordeaux

France's biggest and best-known region for top-quality dryish reds, wines that we call claret. Most of such wines are called Château This or Château That, which will vary from about 60 francs a bottle to the earth and then some. Bordeaux's great white wines are sweet (doux) dessert wines from Sauternes, though there are now some good value dry (sec) wines too.

Bourgogne

We call this small, highly-priced region Burgundy. Its dry whites such as Montrachet are the greatest in the world; its reds can be lovely scented, smooth liquids, though there are some highly-priced disappointments.

Beaujolais/Mâconnais

This is the region just south of Burgundy proper that can offer some less expensive versions of Burgundy's white wines from the vineyards round Mâcon and some easy-drinking, gulpable reds from the vineyards of the Beaujolais area. Drink all these wines young.

Rhône

Mainly red wines and generally very good value. The whites can be quirky and heavy, but there has been a run of extremely good vintages of the meaty or spicy reds.

Loire

France's other great river is best-known, rather neatly, for its white wines – all with lots of acidity and great with food. Most Loire wines are designed for early consumption.

Alsace

France's most overlooked wine region, perhaps because it is almost in Germany. Fragrant, dry whites named after the Germanic grape varieties from which they are made. (This practice, varietal naming, is still uncommon in France though it is gaining ground elsewhere throughout the wine world.)

Since French Entrée territory is so far from France's vine land, the visitor is offered a much more catholic selection of (French) wines than in wine regions further south. The French take chauvinism seriously and on a local scale. Remember that most dry white wines do not improve with age, so don't begrudge being asked to drink a very young vintage. Merely feel grateful that you can enjoy the wine while it's young and fresh. As for matching specific wines with food, I subscribe to the view that you should start by deciding what colour and weight you feel like drinking rather than following the choice dictated by the 'white with fish and red with meat' rule. If you want white with a rich meat dish, it makes sense to choose a full-bodied one such as white burgundy, while light-bodied, fairly tart reds like Beaujolais and Bourgueil make better fish partners than a rich Rhône would.

COMMON WINE TERMS – AN ALPHABETICAL GUIDE

The following are the words most likely to be encountered on labels and wine lists, with brief notes to help you towards the clues they give to what's inside the bottle.

Alsace – Wine region, see above.

Anjou – Loire source of lots of medium rosé and a bit of safe, unexciting dry white.

Appellation Contrôlée – France's top 20 per cent of wine, named after the area where it is made.

Barsac – Sweet white bordeaux. Part of Sauternes so all Barsac is Sauternes but not all Sauternes is Barsac.

Beaujolais – Light, juicy reds.

Beaune – Southern town in the Burgundy heartland. Any wine carrying this name alone will be expensive.

Blanc de Blancs – Sounds fancy but means very little. Literally, a white wine made of white grapes, unusual in a champagne but obvious in a still white.

Bordeaux – Wine region, see above.

Bourgogne – 'Burgundy', a wine region, see above.

Bourgueil (Pronounce 'Boor-gurr-yeh') – Light red from the middle Loire.

Brut – Extremely dry; applies particularly to sparkling wines.

Chablis – A much traduced name. True chablis (and the only sort of chablis you're likely to encounter in France) is steely-dry white burgundy from a village of the same name in the far north of the Burgundy region.

Champagne – Wine region, see above.

Château — Principally refers to Bordeaux wine estate, not necessarily possessing an actual château. Because of the prestige of "château", the title has become abused by dubious "phantom châteaux" labels for very ordinary wines: caveat emptor!

Châteauneuf-du-Pape – Full-bodied spicy red from the southern Rhône.

Chenin (Blanc) – The white grape of the Middle Loire, medium dry usually.

Corbières – Straiahtforward southern red.

Côte(s) de – 'Côte(s) de X' is usually better than a wine named simply 'X', as it means it comes from the (superior) hillsides above the lower ground of the X vineyards.

Coteaux de – Similar to 'Côte(s) de'.

Coteaux d'Ancenis – North Loire VDQS varietal whites. All dry except for Malvoisie.

Coteaux du Languedoc – Lightish southern red.

Coteaux du Layon – Small Middle Loire area producing some excellent but many unexciting medium dry whites.

Coteaux du Tricastin – Lightish version of Côtes-du-Rhône.

Côtes de Provence – Appellation for the dry white, herby red and, principally, dry pink wines of Provence in south-east France.

Côtes-du-Rhône – This big appellation with some new-style dry whites but mainly lightish spicy reds like Châteauneuf is usually good value.

Crozes-Hermitage – Convenient, earlier-maturing but still quite concentrated version of (almost always red) Hermitage.

Cru – Means 'growth' literally, Grand cru means 'great growth' and really rather good. *Cru classé* means that the growth has been officially classified as up to some definite scratch, and most of the world's best clarets are *crus classés*.

Demi-Sec – Literally, medium dry; more likely to mean sweet.

Domaine – Wine estate in Burgundy.

Doux – Sweet.

Entre-Deux Mers – Dry, and rarely exciting, white from Bordeaux.

Fleurie – Single-village beaujolais; superior.

Frappé – Served on crushed ice; e.g. *crème de menthe frappé*.

Gaillac – Inexpensive white and sometimes red from southwest France.

Glacé – Chilled; not the same as *frappé*.

Graves – Red and usually-dry white from a good-value area of Bordeaux.

Gewürztraminer – Perfumed grape grown in Alsace to produce France's most easily-recognisable white wine.

Haut – High or upper; topographical term. It happens that Haut-Médoc produces finer wine than the region's lower vineyards.

Hautes-Côtes de Beaune or Nuits – Affordable red and white burgundy from the slopes, high in altitude but not, for once, necessarily quality.

Hermitage – Long lived tannic red from the northern Rhône.

Juliénas – Single-village beaujolais; superior.

Kir – Chilled dry white wine poured on to a little *crème de cassis* (q.v.). Splendid aperitif. Also Kir *royale* – made with champagne!

Loire – Wine region, see above.

Mâcon – Southern end of Burgundy, source of good-value whites and some unexciting reds.

Margaux – Médoc village producing scented clarets.

méthode champenoise – The Champagne region's way of putting bubbles into wine and usually the sign of a good one.

Meursault – Very respectable burgundy, almost all white.

Minervois – Better-than-average southern red.

mis(e) en bouteilles au château – Bottled at the Château (as opposed to in some merchant's cellars) and usually a sign of quality.

Moelleux – Medium sweet.

Monbazillac – Good-value country cousin to Sauternes.

Montrachet – Very great white burgundy.

Moulin-à-Vent – Single-village beaujolais which, unusually, can be kept.

Mousseux – Sparkling.

Mouton-Cadet – Not a special property, but a commercial blend of claret.

Muscadet – Lean, dry white from the mouth of the Loire. Very tart.

Muscat – The grape whose wines, unusually, taste and smell grapey. Dry in Alsace; very sweet and strong from places like Rivesaltes, Frontignan and Beaumes de Venise.

Nouveau – "New" wine; see *primeur* (the more technical term) – popularised by Beaujolais shippers. Other regions have copied what some experts consider overrated fad.

Nuits-St-Georges – Burgundy's second wine town. Bottles carrying this name are often expensive.

Pauillac – Bordeaux's most famous village, containing three of the five top châteaux. Very aristocratic claret.

Pétillant – Slightly sparkling wine.

Pineau – Unfermented grape juice fortified with grape alcohol: chilled, an interesting aperitif drink. *Pineau des Charentes* best-known.

Pomerol – Soft, fruity claret. Similar to St Emilion.

Pommard – Soft, fruity red burgundy.

Pouilly-Fuissé – Famous appellation in the Mâcon region. Dry, white and sometimes overpriced.

Pouilly-Fumé – Much tarter than Pouilly-Fuissé, made from the Sauvignon grape (see below) in Loire.

Premières Côtes de Bordeaux – Inexpensive red and sweet white bordeaux.

Primeur – Wine designed to be drunk within months of the vintage e.g. from November till Easter. Beaujolais Nouveau is a 'Primeur'.

Puligny-Montrachet – Steely white burgundy and often very good.

Riesling – Germany's famous grape produces great dry wine in Alsace.

Ste-Croix-du-Mont – Inexpensive sweet white bordeaux.

St Emilion – Soft, early-maturing claret from many little properties, most of which seem to be allowed to call themselves *crus classés*.

St Estèphe – Sometimes rather hard but noble claret.

St Julien – Another Médoc village housing many great châteaux.

Sancerre – Twin village to the Pouilly of Pouilly Fumé, and producing very similar wines.

Santenay – Light red burgundy.

Saumur – Town in the middle Loire giving its name to wines of all colours, degrees of sweetness and some very good sparkling wine too.

Sauvignon – Grape producing dry whites with lots of 'bite'.

Savigny-lés-Beaune – Village just outside Beaune responsible for some good-value 'proper' red burgundy.

Sec – Literally "dry", but don't be fooled – usually a sweetish wine.

Supérieur(e) – as Haut (above), and not a qualitative term, an exception being in VDQS (q.v.).

Sylvaner – Alsace's 'everyday' light, dry white. Often the best wine you can buy by the glass in a French bar.

Touraine – An area in the middle Loire producing inexpensive Sauvignon and other wines.

VDQS – *Vin Delimite de Qualite Supérieure* (see above) between AC and Vins de Pays.

Vin de Pays – Quality level at the top end of table wine. Many good-value inexpensive reds and some whites stating their region of origin on the label.

Vin de Pays des Marches de Bretagne – The only wine with an obviously Breton name. Light, tartish, usually white.

Vin de Table – The most basic sort of wine made in France. Very few excitements in this category. The blends with the name of a Burgundy merchant on the label are usually the most expensive.

Volnay – Soft red burgundy.

Xérès – ("ereth"): *vin de Xérès* = sherry.

HINTS ON SPIRITS FROM JOHN DOXAT

The great French spirit is brandy. Cognac, commercially the leader, must come from the closely controlled region of that name. Of various quality designations, the commonest is VSOP (very special old pale): it will be a cognac worth drinking neat. Remember, *champagne* in a cognac connotation has absolutely no connection with the wine. It is a topographical term, *grande champagne* being the most prestigious cognac area: fine champagne is a blend of brandy from the two top cognac sub-divisions.

Armagnac has become better known lately outside France, and rightly so. As a brandy it has a much longer history than cognac: some connoisseurs rate old armagnac (the quality designations are roughly similar) above cognac.

Be cautious of French brandy without a cognac or armagnac title, regardless of how many meaningless "stars" the label carries or even the magic word "Napoleon" (which has no legal significance).

Little appreciated in Britain is the splendid "apple brandy", Calvados, mainly associated with Normandy but also made in Brittany and the Marne. The best is Calvados *du Pays d'Auge*. Do taste well aged Calvados, but avoid any suspiciously cheap.

Contrary to popular belief, true Calvados is not distilled from cider- but an inferior imitation is: French cider (*cidre*) is excellent.

Though most French proprietary aperitifs, like Dubonnet, are fairly low in alcohol, the extremely popular Pernod/ Ricard *pastis*-style brands are highly spirituous. *Eau-de-vie* is the generic term for all spirits, but colloquially tends to refer to, often rough, local distillates. An exception are the better *alcools blancs* (white spirits), which are not inexpensive, made from fresh fruits and not sweetened as *crèmes* are.

Liqueurs

Numerous travellers deem it worth allocating their allowance to bring back some of the famous French liqueurs (Bénédictine, Chartreuse, Cointreau, and so on) which are so costly in Britain. Compare "duty free" prices with those in stores, which can vary markedly. There is a plethora of regional liqueurs, and numerous sickly *crèmes*, interesting to taste locally. The only *crème* generally meriting serious consideration as a liqueur is *crème de menthe* (preferably Cusenier), though the newish *crème de Grand Marnier* has been successful . *Crème de cassis* has a special function: see Kir in alphabetical list.

Glossary of cooking terms and dishes

(It would take another book to list comprehensively French cooking terms and dishes, but here are the ones most likely to be encountered.)

Aigre-doux	bittersweet
Aiguillette	thin slice (*aiguille* – needle)
Aile	wing
Aiolli	garlic mayonnaise
Allemande (à l')	German style, i.e.: with sausages and sauerkraut
Amuse-gueules	appetisers
Anglaise (à l')	plain boiled. *Crème Anglaise* – egg and cream sauce
Andouille	large uncooked sausage, served cold after boiling
Andouillettes	ditto but made from smaller intestines, usually served hot after grilling
Anis	aniseed
Argenteuil	with asparagus
Assiette Anglaise	plate of cold meats
Baba au rhum	yeast-based sponge macerated in rum
Baguette	long, thin loaf
Ballotine	boned, stuffed and rolled meat or poultry, usually cold
Béarnaise	sauce made from egg yolks, butter, tarragon, wine, shallots
Beurre blanc	sauce from Nantes, with butter, reduction of shallot-flavoured vinegar or wine
Béchamel	white sauce flavoured with infusion of herbs
Beignets	fritters
Bercy	sauce with white wine and shallots
Beurre noir	browned butter
Bigarade	with oranges
Billy By	mussel soup
Bisque	creamy shellfish soup
Blanquette	stew with thick, white creamy sauce, usually veal
Boeuf à la mode	braised beef
Bombe	ice-cream mould
Bonne femme	with root vegetables
Bordelais	Bordeaux-style, with red or white wine, marrowbone fat
Bouchée	mouthful, e.g. vol-au-vent
Boudin	sausage, white or black
Bourride	thick fish-soup
Braisé	braised
Court-bouillon	aromatic liquor for cooking meat, fish, vegetables
Couscous	N. African dish with millet, chicken, vegetable variations
Crapaudine	involving fowl, particularly pigeon, trussed

Brandade (de morue	dried salt-cod pounded into a mousse
Broche	spit
Brochette	skewer
Brouillade	stew, using oil
Brouillé	scrambled
Brûlé	burnt, e.g. *crème brûlée*
Campagne	country style
Cannelle	cinnamon
Carbonnade	braised in beer
Cardinal	red-coloured sauce, e.g. with lobster, or in *pâtisserie* with redcurrant
Cassolette or cassoulette	small pan
Cassoulet	rich stew with goose, pork and haricot beans
Cervelas	pork garlic sausage
Cervelles	brains
Chantilly	whipped sweetened cream
Charcuterie	cold pork-butcher's meats
Charlotte	mould, as dessert lined with sponge-fingers, as savoury lined with vegetable
Chasseur	with mushrooms, shallots, wine
Chausson	pastry turnover
Chemise	covering, i.e. pastry
Chiffonade	thinly-cut, e.g. lettuce
Choron	tomato Béarnaise
Choucroute	Alsatian stew with sauerkraut and sausages
Civet	stew
Clafoutis	batter dessert, usually with cherries
Clamart	with peas
Cocotte	covered casserole
Cocque (à la)	e.g. *oeufs* – boiled eggs
Compôte	cooked fruit
Concassé	e.g. *tomates concassées* – skinned, chopped, juice extracted
Confit	preserved
Confiture	jam
Consommé	clear soup
Cou	neck
Coulis	juice, purée (of vegetables or fruit)
Galette	Breton pancake, flat cake
Garbure	thick country soup
Garni	garnished, usually with vegetables
Gaufre	waffle
Gelée	aspic

Crécy	with carrots
Crème pâtissière	thick custard filling
Crêpe	pancake
Crépinette	little flat sausage, encased in caul
Croque-Monsieur	toasted cheese-and-ham sandwich
Croustade	pastry or baked bread shell
Croûte	pastry crust
Croûton	cube of fried or toasted bread
Cru	raw
Crudités	raw vegetables
Demi-glâce	basic brown sauce
Doria	with cucumber
Émincé	thinly sliced
Étuvé	stewed, e.g. vegetables in butter
Entremets	sweets
Farci	stuffed
Fines herbes	parsley, thyme, bayleaf
Feuilleté	leaves of flaky pastry
Flamande	Flemish style, with beer
Flambé	flamed in spirit
Flamiche	flan
Florentine	with spinach
Flûte	thinnest bread loaf
Foie gras	goose liver
Fondu	melted
Fond (d'artichaut)	heart (of artichoke)
Forestière	with mushrooms, bacon and potatoes
Four (au)	baked in the oven
Fourré	stuffed, usually sweets
Fricandeau	veal, usually topside
Frais, fraîche	fresh and cool
Frangipane	almond-cream pâtisserie
Fricadelle	Swedish meat ball
Fricassé	(usually of veal) in creamy sauce
Frit	fried
Frites	chips
Friture	assorted small fish, fried in batter
Froid	cold
Fumé	smoked
Galantine	loaf-shaped chopped meat, fish or vegetable, set in natural jelly
Marinière	seamens' style e.g. moules marinière (mussels in white wine)
Marmite	deep casserole
Matelote	fish stew, e.g. of eel
Médaillon	round slice
Melange	mixture

Gésier	gizzard
Gibier	game
Gigot	leg
Glacé	iced
Gougère	choux pastry, large base
Goujons	fried strips, usually of fish
Graine	seed
Gratin	baked dish of vegetables cooked in cream and eggs
Gratinée	browned under grill
Grecque (à la)	cold vegetables served in oil
Grenadin	nugget of meat, usually of veal
Grenouilles	frogs; cuisses de grenouille – frogs' legs
Grillé	grilled
Gros sel	coarse salt
Hachis	minced or chopped
Haricot	slow cooked stew
Hochepot	hotpot
Hollandaise	sauce with egg, butter, lemon
Hongroise	Hungarian, i.e. spiced with paprika
Hors-d'oeuvre	assorted starters
Huile	oil
Île flottante	floating island – soft meringue on egg-custard sauce
Indienne	Indian, i.e. with hot spices
Jambon	ham
Jardinière	from the garden, i.e. with vegetables
Jarret	shin, e.g. jarret de veau
Julienne	matchstick vegetables
Jus	natural juice
Lait	milk
Langue	tongue
Lard	bacon
Longe	loin
Macédoine	diced fruits or vegetables
Madeleine	small sponge cake
Magret	breast (of duck)
Maïs	sweetcorn
Maître d'hôtel	sauce with butter, lemon, parsley
Marchand de vin	sauce with red wine, shallots
Marengo	sauce with tomatoes, olive oil, white wine
Pot-au-four	broth with meat and vegetables
Potée	country soup with cabbage
Pralines	caramelised almonds
Primeurs	young veg
Printanier (printanière)	garnished with early vegetables

Meunière	sauce with butter, lemon	*Profiteroles*	choux pastry balls
Miel	honey	*Provençale*	with garlic, tomatoes, olive oil, peppers
Mille-feuille	flaky pastry, (lit. 1,000 leaves)		
Mirepoix	cubed carrot, onion etc. used for sauces	*Pureé*	mashed and sieved
Moëlle	beef marrow	*Quenelle*	pounded fish or meat bound with egg, poached
Mornay	cheese sauce		
Mouclade	mussel stew	*Queue*	tail
Mousseline	Hollandaise sauce, lightened with egg whites	*Quiche*	pastry flan, e.g. *quiche Lorraine* – egg, bacon, cream
Moutarde	mustard		
		Râble	saddle, e.g. *râble de lièvre*
Nage (à la)	poached in flavoured liquor (fish)	*Ragoût*	stew
		Ramequin	little pot
Nature	plain	*Râpé*	grated
Navarin (d'agneau)	stew of lamb with spring vegetables	*Ratatouille*	Provençale stew of onions, garlic, peppers, tomatoes
Noisette	nut-brown, burned butter	*Ravigote*	highly seasoned white sauce
Noix de veau	nut (leg) of veal	*Rémoulade*	mayonnaise with gherkins, capers, herbs and shallots
Normande	Normandy style, i.e. with cream, apple, cider, Calvados	*Rillettes*	potted shredded meat, usually fat pork or goose
Nouilles	noodles		
		Riz	rice
Onglet	beef cut from flank	*Robert*	sauce with mustard, vinegar, onion
Os	bone		
		Roquefort	ewe's milk blue cheese
Paillettes	straws (of pastry)	*Rossini*	garnished with foie gras and truffle
Panaché	mixed		
Panade	flour crust	*Rôti*	roast
Papillote (en)	cooked in paper case	*Rouelle*	nugget
Parmentier	with potatoes	*Rouille*	hot garlicky sauce for *soupe de poisson*
Pâté	paste, of meat or fish		
Pâte	pastry	*Roulade*	roll
Pâté brisée	rich short-crust pastry	*Roux*	sauce base – flour and butter
Pâtisserie	pastries		
Paupiettes	paper-thinslice	*Sabayon*	sweet fluffy sauce, with eggs and wine
Pavé	thick slice		
Paysan	country style	*Safran*	saffron
Périgueux	with truffles	*Sagou*	sago
Persillade	chopped parsley and garlic topping	*St-Germain*	with peas
		Salade niçoise	with tunny, anchovies, tomatoes, beans, black olives
Petits fours	tiny cakes, sweetmeats		
Petit pain	bread roll	*Salé*	salted
Piperade	peppers, onions, tomatoes in scrambled egg	*Salmis*	dish of game or fowl, with red wine
Poché	poached	*Sang*	blood
Poêlé	fried	*Santé*	lit. healthy, i.e. with spinach and potato
Poitrine	breast		
Poivre	pepper	*Salpicon*	meat, fowl, vegetables, chopped fine, bound with sauce and used as fillings
Pommade	paste		
Potage	thick soup		
Saucisse	fresh sausage	*Thé*	tea
Saucisson	dried sausage	*Tiède*	luke warm
Sauté	cooked in fat in open pan	*Timbale*	steamed mould
Sauvage	wild	*Tisane*	infusion
Savarin	ring of yeast-sponge, soaked in syrup and liquor	*Tourte*	pie
		Tranche	thick slice
Sel	salt	*Truffes*	truffles
Selle	saddle	*Tuile*	tile, i.e. thin biscuit

Selon	according to, e.g. *selon grosseur* (according to size)	*Vacherin*	meringue confection
Smitane	with sour cream, white wine, onion	*Vallée d'Auge*	with cream, apple, Calvados
		Vapeur (au)	steamed
Soissons	with dried white beans	*Velouté*	white sauce, bouillon-flavoured
Sorbet	water ice		
Soubise	with creamed onions	*Véronique*	with grapes
Soufflé	puffed, i.e. mixed with egg white and baked	*Vert(e)*	green, e.g. *sauce verte*, with herbs
Sucre	sugar (*sucré* – sugared)	*Vessie*	pig's bladder
Suprême	fillet of poultry breast or fish	*Vichysoise*	chilled creamy leek and potato soup
Tartare	raw minced beef, flavoured with onions etc. and bound with raw egg	*Vierge*	prime olive oil
		Vinaigre	vinegar (lit. bitter wine)
		Vinaigrette	wine vinegar and oil dressing
Tartare (sauce)	mayonnaise with capers, herbs, onions	*Volaille*	poultry
		Vol-au-vent	puff-pastry case
Tarte Tatin	upside down apple pie		
Terrine	pottery dish/baked minced, chopped meat, veg., chicken, fish or fruit	*Xérès*	sherry
		Yaourt	yoghurt

FISH – Les Poissons, SHELLFISH – Les Coquillages

Alose	shad	*Daurade*	sea bream
Anchois	anchovy	*Écrevisse*	crayfish
Anguille	eel	*Éperlan*	smelt
Araignée de mer	spider crab	*Espadon*	swordfish
		Étrille	baby crab
Bar	sea bass	*Favouille*	spider crab
Barbue	brill	*Flétan*	halibut
Baudroie	monkfish, anglerfish	*Fruits de mer*	seafood
Belon	oyster – flat shelled	*Grondin*	red gurnet
Bigorneau	winkle	*Hareng*	herring
Blanchaille	whitebait	*Homard*	lobster
Brochet	pike	*Huître*	oyster
Cabillaud	cod	*Julienne*	ling
Calamar	squid	*Laitance*	soft herring-roe
Carpe	carp	*Lamproie*	lamprey
Carrelet	plaice	*Langouste*	spring lobster, or crawfish
Chapon de mer	scorpion fish	*Langoustine*	Dublin Bay prawn
Claire	oyster	*Lieu*	ling
Coquille St-Jacques	scallop	*Limand*	lemon sole
		Lotte de mer	monkfish
Crabe	crab	*Loup de mer*	sea bass
Crevette grise	shrimp	*Maquereau*	mackerel
Crevette rose	prawn	*Merlan*	whiting
Morue	salt cod	*St-Pierre*	John Dory
Moule	mussel	*Sandre*	zander
Mulet	grey mullet	*Saumon*	salmon
Ombre	grayling	*Saumonette*	rock salmon
Oursin	sea urchin	*Seiche*	squid
Palourde	clam	*Sole*	sole
Pétoncle	small scallop	*Soupion*	inkfish
Plie	plaice	*Thon*	tunny
Portugaise	oyster	*Tortue*	turtle
Poulpe	octopus	*Torteau*	large crab

Praire	oyster	Truite	trout
Raie	skate	Turbot	turbot
Rascasse	scorpion-fish	Turbotin	chicken turbot
Rouget	red mullet		

FRUITS – Les Fruits, VEGETABLES – Les Légumes, NUTS – Les Noix

HERBS – Les Herbes, SPICES – Les Épices

Ail	garlic	Courgette	courgette
Algue	seaweed	Cresson	watercress
Amande	almond	Échalote	shallot
Ananas	pineapple	Endive	chicory
Aneth	dill	Épinard	spinach
Abricot	apricot	Escarole	salad leaves
Arachide	peanut	Estragon	tarragon
Artichaut	globe artichoke	Fenouil	fennel
Asperge	asparagus	Fève	broad bean
Avocat	avocado	Flageolet	dried bean
Banane	banana	Fraise	strawberry
Basilic	basil	Framboise	raspberry
Betterave	beetroot	Genièvre	juniper
Blette	Swiss chard	Gingembre	ginger
Brugnon	nectarine	Girofle	clove
Cassis	blackcurrant	Girolle	edible fungus
Céléri	celery	Grenade	pomegranate
Céléri-rave	celeriac	Griotte	bitter red cherry
Cêpe	edible fungus	Groseille	gooseberry
Cerfeuil	chervil	Groseille noire	blackcurrant
Cerise	cherry	Groseille rouge	redcurrant
Champignon	mushroom	Haricot	dried white bean
Chanterelle	edible fungus	Haricot vert	French bean
Châtaigne	chestnut	Laitue	lettuce
Chicorée	endive	Mandarine	tangerine, mandarin
Chou	cabbage	Mangetout	sugar pea
Chou-fleur	cauliflower	Marron	chestnut
Choux de Bruxelles	Brussels sprouts	Menthe	mint
		Mirabelle	tiny gold plum
Ciboulette	chive	Morille	dark brown crinkly edioble fungus
Citron	lemon		
Citron vert	lime	Mûre	blackberry
Coing	quince	Muscade	nutmeg
Concombre	cucumber	Myrtille	bilberry, blueberry
Coriandre	coriander	Navet	turnip
Cornichon	gherkin	Noisette	hazelnut
Courge	pumpkin	Oignon	onion
Oseille	sorrel	Pomme	apple
Palmier	palm	Pomme de terre	potato
Pamplemousse	grapefruit	Prune	plum
Panais	parsnip	Pruneau	prune
Passe-Pierre	seaweed	Quetsch	small dark plum
Pastèque	water melon	Radis	radish
Peche	peach	Raifort	horseradish
Persil	parsley	Raisin	grape
Petit pois	pea	Reine Claude	greengage
Piment doux	sweet pepper	Romarin	rosemary
Pissenlit	dandelion	Safran	saffron

Pistache	pistachio	Salsifis	salsify
Pleurote	edible fungi	Thym	thyme
Poire	pear	Tilleul	lime blossom
Poireau	leek	Tomate	tomato
Poivre	pepper	Topinambour	Jerusalem artichoke
Poivron	green, red and yellow peppers	Truffe	truffle

MEAT – Les Viandes

Le Boeuf	Beef	Le Porc	Pork
Charolais	is the best	Jambon	ham
Chateaubriand	double fillet steak	Jambon cru	raw smoked ham
Contrefilet	sirloin	Porcelet	suckling pig
Entrecôte	rib steak		
Faux Filet	sirloin steak	Le Veau	Veal
Filet	fillet	Escalope	thin slice cut from fillet
L'Agneau	Lamb	Les Abats	Offal
Pré-Salé	is the best	Foie	liver
Carré	neck cutlets	Foie gras	goose liver
Côte	chump chop	Cervelles	brains
Epaule	shoulder	Langue	tongue
Gigot	leg	Ris	sweetbreads
		Rognons	kidneys
		Tripes	tripe

POULTRY – Volaille, GAME – Gibier

Abatis	giblets	Lièvre	hare
Bécasse	woodcock	Oie	goose
Bécassine	snipe	Perdreau	partridge
Caille	quail	Pigeon	pigeon
Canard	duck	Pintade	guineafowl
Caneton	duckling	Pluvier	plover
Chapon	capon	Poularde	chicken (boiling)
Chevreuil	roe deer	Poulet	chicken (roasting)
Dinde	young hen turkey	Poussin	spring chicken
Dindon	turkey	Sanglier	wild boar
Dindonneau	young turkey	Sarcelle	teal
Faisan	pheasant	Venaison	venison
Grive	thrush		

Index

Other Entrée Guides

French Entrée 5	Brittany	£6.95
French Entrée 6	Coast to Capital – Boulogne, Pays d'Opale, Picardy	£6.95
French Entrée 8	The Loire	£6.95
French Entrée 9	Normandy Encore	£6.95
French Entrée 10	South of France	£6.95
French Entrée 11	Paris	£6.95
French Entrée 13	Provence	£6.95
Entrée to Malta		£6.95
Entrée to Mallorca		£6.95

Coming

French Entrée 12	The North of France	£6.95
Entrée to the Algarve		£6.95

In preparation:

FRENCH ENTRÉE 14 Dordogne
ENTRÉE TO TUSCANY
ENTRÉE TO FLORIDA   and many others

– a companion to French Entrée to help you enjoy your holiday more.

LEGAL BEAGLE GOES TO FRANCE
Bill Thomas £3.95
All you need to deal with problems involving the law in France – accidents, houses, travel – even births and deaths. Includes: legal and customs formalities; daily life in France; eating, sleeping and drinking; en route; getting around without a car; renting a gîlte and buying a house.

Also published by Quiller Press

SPAIN BY CAR
Norman Renouf £7.95
The essential guide to food and accommodation for all
motorists in Spain. Objective information and photographs of
over 650 hotels, guest houses, motels and hostels along the
main roads.

WALES – A GOOD EATING GUIDE
Roger Thomas £5.95
A guide for tourists and locals alike, to nearly 300 restaurants
and shops recommended for typically Welsh food. Inside
information on where to eat in Wales, with a map and 40 line
drawings.

INVITATION TO DEVON
Joy David £6.95
Places to visit, eat and sleep throughout the county, by a
devoted Devonian. With over 100 line drawings.

EVERYBODY'S HISTORIC LONDON
Jonathan Kiek £6.95
Historian and teacher Jonathan Kiek's award-winning guide to
London is now in its fourth edition. 60 photographs, maps and
plans complement background history and up-to-date
practical information.

EVERYBODY'S HISTORIC ENGLAND
Jonathan Kiek £6.95
Much-praised combination of popular history and carefully
thought-out tours of the whole of England – required reading
for all travellers who enjoy our national heritage.

WINDOW ON GOA
Maurice Hall £16.95
An in-depth history and guide to this tropical paradise. Over
200 colour pictures and over 100,000 words. Casebound.

Please order from your bookshop or, in case of difficulty, write
with payment to:
Quiller Press, 46 Lillie Road, London SW6 1TN.

Notes